Teaching Musicianship in the High School Band

JOSEPH A. LABUTA

PARKER PUBLISHING COMPANY, INC.

West Nyack, N. Y.

Respectfully dedicated to three master teachers of musicianship:

Charles Leonhard,
Hubert Kessler, and
Charles Winking.

© 1972 By

Parker Publishing Company, Inc.

West Nyack, N.Y.

Library of Congress
Catalog Card Number: 70-157720

Printed in The United States of America

ISBN 0-13-892679-4
B&P

How This Book Will Improve Your
Teaching - And Your Band

The purpose of this book is to offer specific suggestions to school band directors for developing the musicianship of their band members. Musicians seem to know intuitively what musicianship means and use the term in varying contexts. Music theory courses are labeled in many college catalogs as "courses in musicianship." Certainly all theory and history courses should have the improvement of musicianship as a broad aim. On the other hand, the term musicianship is often used when referring to comprehensive musical attributes and abilities of performers. It is theory applied to practice; it is knowledge and skill applied to practical music making. Musicianship is used here in the latter sense.

To teach musicianship you must consistently emphasize and explain the relationship of structure and style to performance. The first step is to develop a band curriculum emphasizing music as a fine art or cultural, aesthetic study. This results in a music appreciation course for band—"Music Appreciation"—of the highest quality, not the usual, degrading connotation. Aesthetic education is currently advocated as a goal for all school music groups and classes. Performance provides a most effective medium to teach aesthetic sensitivity and understanding.

The band director's choice of music is critical. It is far from redundant to say that the director must put *music* into the band program—quality literature, plus knowledge of its structure and style.

The highest attainable level of performance is necessary. By planning carefully, nothing is lost in the quality of performance. In fact, students should perform better because they understand what they are doing and why they are doing it. Many directors of first division groups spend up to one-fifth of their rehearsal time teaching musical content to their students.[1]

However, only spurious learnings can accrue through an inconsistent approach. The director must be organized and consistent to teach musicianship effectively. Since few materials for teaching musicianship are available for use by busy band directors, programs remain too performance oriented.

This book provides a broad curriculum outline or guide for the director. He can use it in its entirety in the sequence presented, or he can use separate chapters as units of study. Valid musical examples are used representing several levels of difficulty. These are an excellent source of quality literature for programming. Lecture and resource materials are given on timbre, structural elements, form, styles and performance. Specific illustrations are provided from the literature to be played by the band. The band, then, becomes a seminar or workshop with members as active participants. Methods of presentation and evaluative techniques are also provided.

---

[1] See the following articles: Richard E. Papke, "Directors: Take Time to Teach and Evaluate," *The Instrumentalist*, May, 1966, p. 40 ; Richard E. Papke, "Music Education—Not Just Performance," *The Instrumentalist*, January, 1968, p. 44 ; Victor Bordo, "Music History Through Band Literature," *Music Journal*, Vol. XXVII, No. 10, December, 1969, p. 36. Other directors teaching "content" in performance groups can be found in *Music in General Education*. (Washington D.C.: Music Educator's National Conference, 1965), pp. 197-9.

A curriculum based upon the suggestions contained in this book provides a sound justification for the band program. Valid literature is presented with strategies to foster theoretical, stylistic and discriminative learnings based upon this literature. As a practical outcome, it is hoped that the proposed curriculum should help the band achieve the status of a "solid" subject. At least, additional credit and prestige would be warranted. Rather than administrators easing band from the curriculum, band should retain or regain its position as part of the regular school day. A curriculum of this type would also answer the criticism of administrators who argue that the band program really has no "content" since a student does essentially the same thing from one year to the next. For this reason the student can be counselled to drop band for a more "important" subject in his junior or senior year with little harm to his basic musical education. Instead, a carefully planned curriculum should help ally the band and administration. In a similar way, I have experienced a positive change in the attitude of classroom teachers toward band when they became aware that students learn significant content of cultural value. Finally, graduates from the proposed curriculum should not be as musically illiterate as those from exclusively performance oriented programs.

The success of the program ultimately depends upon the band director who is enthusiastic about teaching good music to his students.

Joseph A. Labuta

Contents

How This Book Will Improve Your Teaching—and Your Band · 7

. *How to Select and Present Music for Teaching Musicianship* · 15

Selecting Music

Time and Scheduling Problems (Warm-up and Tuning, Ensemble Drill, Rehearsal Management)

How to Present Music (Provide Incidental Information, Distribute Printed Material, Prepare Program Notes, Assign Out-of-Class Study, Utilize Class, Provide Music Subject Electives)

Long Range Continuity

The Conductor as Teacher

Content and Organization of the Chapters

2. How to Teach Timbre and Improve Band Sound · 27

Improving Individual Tone Quality in Rehearsal
Try a Tone Improvement Workshop
Improving Sonority in the Band
The Small Ensemble Program and Tone
Assisting Student Arrangers
A Project for Teaching Timbre
Other Projects

3. How to Teach the Musical Elements: Rhythm · 42

Teaching Beat and Meter (Beat, Meter, Polymeter, Uneven
    Meter, Changing Meters, Nonmetric Music)
Reading and Interpreting Rhythms (Feeling Beat Units,
    Counting Divisions and Subdivisions of the Beat, Achieving
    Rhythmic Flow, Achieving Evenness of Runs)
Teaching Rhythms in Rehearsal (Sight Reading Experience,
    Demonstration, Analysis and Drill Experience)

*4. How to Teach the Musical Elements: Melody and
Theme · 60*

Tonality
Scales (Student Projects, Rehearsal Procedures)
Motive
Sequence
Phrase
Diatonic Structure and Melodic Design
Chromatic Melody
Serial Melody
Theme

*5. How to Teach the Musical Elements: Harmony and Tex-
ture · 72*

Tonality and Chord Construction
Cadence
Dissonance and Consonance
Progression
Contemporary Harmonic Techniques (Polytonality, Serial
    Harmony, Other Harmonic Devices)
Texture (Monophonic Texture, Homophonic Texture, Poly-
    phonic Texture, The Use of Several Textures in One
    Composition)

6. How to Illustrate Structure and Formal Types · *86*

Components and Principles of Form (Design, Tonal Structure)
Teaching Formal Types (Binary Forms, Ternary Forms, Rondo, Theme and Variations, Sonata-allegro, Ostinato Forms, Fugue, Concerto Grosso, Other Forms)
How to Analyze Music (Analytical Procedure)

7. How to Enhance Musicianship by Teaching General Styles of Music · *114*

Articulation and Style
Basic Styles of Music
Specific Methods for Teaching Basic Styles
Study the Symbols of Style
How to Teach March Style
Teaching Rubato Style

8. How to Teach Historical Styles: Performance Practice · *124*

Defining and Explaining Performance Practice (How to Play the Baroque Style, How to Play the Classical Style, How to Play the Romantic Style, How to Play the Contemporary Style)
Projects Comparing Performance Practices (The Dramatic Overture Through the Ages, The March Through the Ages, The Concerto-Grosso Then and Now, The Prelude and Fugue, Then and Now)

9. How to Teach the Historical Styles: Musical Characteristics · *134*

The Baroque Era [c. 1600-1750] (General Characteristics, Melody, Harmony, Rhythm and Articulation, Dynamics, Texture, Instrumentation, Ornamentation, Form, Important Composers, Projects)
The Classical Era [c. 1750-1820] (General Characteristics, Melody, Harmony, Rhythm and Articulation, Dynamics, Texture, Instrumentation, Ornamentation, Form, Important Composers, Compositions)
The Romantic Era [c. 1820-1900] (General Characteristics, Melody, Harmony, Rhythm and Articulation, Dynamics, Texture, Instrumentation, Form, Important Composers, Compositions, Projects)

9. How to Teach the Historical Styles: Musical Characteristics (cont.)

The Contemporary Period [c. 1900-to the Present] (General Characteristics, Melody, Harmony, Rhythm, Dynamics, Texture, Instrumentation, Form, Composers, Trends, and Compositions, Projects)

10. How to Teach The Historical Styles: Comparing Musical Characteristics · 162

Projects Comparing Elements and Forms (Classical Compared to Romantic, Haydn, *London Symphony* and Schubert, *Unfinished* Symphony, Baroque Compared to Classical)

11. How to Teach Musicianship Through Interpreting the Score · 186

Expression Marks (Rehearsal Follow-Up)
Musical Structure and Interpretation (The Nature of Musical Expression, Teaching Phrase and "Line")

12. How to Develop Musical Discrimination in the Student · 200

Judging Performance (Tone, Intonation Technique, Balance, Interpretation, Musical Effect, Other Factors)
Judging Interpretation of Historical Styles
Value Judgments of Music (Peer Culture Music, Band Transcriptions, Criteria for Evaluating Band Music)

13. How to Evaluate Musicianship · 211

Information Examinations (Styles, Form, Fundamentals and Elements of Music, Timbre and Instrumentation, Performance, Expressive Elements)
Listening Examinations
Performance Scales
Out-of-Class Tests and Reports
Individual Performance Tests

14. How to Sell a Musicianship Program to the Administration and Students · 220

Selling the Program to the Administration (The Music Appreciation Assembly, The Music Appreciation Concert)
Selling the Program to Students

Index · 226

1

How to Select and Present Music for Teaching Musicianship

This book provides a comprehensive program for teaching musicianship in the full band rehearsal. The approach is based upon quality band literature which exemplifies the forms and styles of our great musical heritage. To teach musicianship in rehearsal, the director must consistently emphasize—explain and demonstrate—the relationship of music's structure and style to performance. Lecture and resource materials are provided for this purpose.

The book is organized as a curriculum outline or guide that can be followed in the sequence presented. There is a logical order that begins with the study of timbre and structural elements, and progresses through musical form to a chronological presentation of historical styles. Finally, principles of interpretation and standards of performance are examined.

The approach to the materials can be much more flexible, however. The director may choose to use a section, several sections or any chapter as a unit of study. For example, one possible project might be "the style and forms of the Baroque era."

In general, think of the total presentation as a "menu," rather than as a "prescription." It is impossible to prescribe the exact materials and procedures that are "right" and usable in every type of teaching situation. Instead, as from a menu, the director can pick and choose what fits his particular program. In addition, the director can devise his own materials and procedures using the guidelines provided by the suggested curriculum outline.

SELECTING MUSIC

Carefully selected band literature is the foundation of the proposed program. We must put good *music* into the band program in order to teach musicianship. Band literature is the basic material through which musicianship is developed. Students study the "content" of the music they are rehearsing and performing. Thus, not any music will do. It must be quality literature that illustrates the concept to be learned. The music presents the problems; the solutions develop musicianship.

The suggested band literature has been chosen for its musical worth, stylistic validity, teaching potential, and suitability for programming. Learning about the music being rehearsed in no way precludes a culminating performance. Concerts, after all, should be a logical outgrowth of classroom learning. The rehearsal becomes a seminar in which the students learn about the music they are playing. Students should perform better, also, because they understand what they are doing and why they are doing it.

Remember the "menu principle" previously stated. The musical examples included herein are illustrative rather than all-inclusive. Use everything that fits your program. However, search out from all sources any music that is appropriate for your group that illustrates the concepts to be learned. The one necessary condition is that musical examples, from the band literature that students are rehearsing and programming, serve as illustrations for teaching about tone color, structural elements, forms and historical styles.

TIME AND SCHEDULING PROBLEMS

Skeptical directors may well ask, "How can a program of musicianship training work for my band? It sounds fine, but seems rather idealistic, since I hardly have time in my crowded and inadequate rehearsal schedule to prepare for all my public appearances." The immediate answer is to start somewhere. Use what seems practical in your situation. In the final analysis, planning and effective rehearsal management are the keys.

Many authorities advocate and many band directors use a daily rehearsal plan to assure maximum efficiency for limited rehearsal time. A typical fifty-five minute rehearsal routine follows:

Five minutes	Warm-up and tune.
Five minutes	Drill technique and rhythms.
Twenty minutes	Rehearse and "polish" music previously presented.
Twenty minutes	Sight read and rehearse new music.
Five minutes	Provide a pleasant closing—Play a well-liked, well-rehearsed or popular composition.

A plan such as this can be adapted quite readily to the musicianship program. Remember, however, if the study of "musicianship" is to improve performance, this study must be related *directly* to the music being rehearsed and performed. Therefore, give careful consideration to the "warm-up" and "drill" periods.

Warm-up and tuning

Often a chorale or a B-flat scale is used to warm up and tune the band. Both can be effective if students thoroughly understand their purpose. Playing a chorale or any slow passage allows students to listen for tone quality, balance, blend, *and* intonation as they warm up their embouchures and instruments. But this does not happen automatically. Students must be directed to listen, and be told exactly what to listen for in the music. Furthermore, tuning must continue throughout the rehearsal because young players must be reminded to listen and tune at all times. Students also tend to tune differently than they play. They are cold and nervous at the beginning of the period and tend to "pinch." They must be warmed up and relaxed as they play a tuning note. Taking a chord from the music being rehearsed provides an opportunity to do all of the above, and in addition learn something about musical structure.

The customary playing of scales for warm-up and tuning often results in wasted effort also. Try asking your students why they should practice scales. How many will answer in the following ways? (1) "To learn tonality (key feeling) as it relates to the music I play. This helps me to play the right notes and play them better in tune." (2) "To learn the tendencies of active and passive scale tones for more expressive playing." (3) "To gain technical facility since most technically difficult passages in tonal music are based upon scale-wise figures and runs." All of the preceding gets to the heart of musicianship.

Ensemble drill

Unison drill and even individual part drill must be included in the regular rehearsal period if sectional rehearsals cannot be scheduled. As a rule, try to relate drills to the whole group and *always* relate drills to the music being played. To illustrate: don't study one scale or key and then practice music in another key; don't discuss one form or style and then play another; don't study a rhythm from a drill book and then play a composition that does not use that rhythm. Instead, pull drill materials from the music being performed rather than from drill books of unrelated exercises. This is a direct reversal of the usual "drill period" approach, but most effective for learning. For example, the dotted-eighth and sixteenth rhythm is difficult for most young groups to execute accurately. They seem to inevitably slip into a triplet feeling. Unison drill should be used *every* time this rhythm is found in the music being played until it is played correctly. Use the scale based upon the tonality of the composition and play the rhythm on each scale step or repeat it on the tonic.

But do not misunderstand. Technical drill books are valuable for reference since they isolate and attack many of the most common problems. Assign dotted rhythms and other rhythm patterns when they are not correctly played in rehearsal. Select, assign and play scale exercises, arpeggios and chords in the keys of the compositions being rehearsed that day. Technique books have another advantage. Parts are transposed. Therefore, students playing transposing instruments do not have to relate everything the director says from the concert pitch to their instruments. They simply read the correct part. Similarly, bass clef instruments do not have to adjust from written treble notation. However, the basic premise is not altered—the actual problems should derive from, and relate back to, the music being performed for learning to be most efficient and relevant. Find corresponding drills in the technique books that are kept for handy reference and study.

Rehearsal management

Efficient management saves time and provides opportunities to teach musicianship. Outline your rehearsal on the chalkboard. List the order of music. Write out drill materials. Provide important information for students on study sheets. Have examples available for teaching musical concepts. Prepare or secure audio-visual aids.

In the next section, procedures are suggested to implement a musicianship program. Each approach is related to the traditional rehearsal routine and its modifications as developed in this section.

HOW TO PRESENT MUSIC

The director can use several procedures to present music to teach musicianship in rehearsal. He can (1) provide incidental information, (2) distribute printed materials, (3) prepare program notes, (4) assign out-of-class study, (5) utilize class discussion, and (6) provide additional music courses. Perhaps it is superficial to list these procedures as separate and exclusive approaches since they can be used most effectively in combination as well as singly. However, for the sake of complete presentation, the characteristics, values and limitations of each method are discussed to help the director ascertain which are appropriate to his teaching situation.

Provide incidental information

In this approach, the director relates incidental information about the music as the rehearsal progresses. Stylistic, analytical, and historical facts, dates, and other anecdotal data are tossed out to the group. Most directors seem to do this as a normal part of day by day teaching. The following examples illustrate:

> "A fugue has a series of entrances of the theme or 'subject' in different voices. This is called 'imitation.' Watch balance! Be sure to drop back at least one dynamic level when a new voice enters so it can be heard."
>
> "The music is by Mozart. It is light, gay and well articulated. Play it accordingly."
>
> "Listen to this recording of the composition to check rhythm and phrasing. Note the tone quality of the professionals also."

While this type of information may be very pertinent to the composition at hand, it may have little carry-over to future music making. Unrelated facts lack continuity and meaning, and are usually forgotten by the students. However, this need not be the case. Incidental information that is consciously related to concepts studied earlier—that clarifies or reviews earlier learning, and deepens meaning—will tend to be remembered.

The rehearsal plan that is appropriate for this model of learning is the same as for any rehearsal. Information is given in those places where normal breaks occur in the rehearsal. Such breaks include rest periods between musical selections, and stops where other suggestions or corrections are made.

Distribute printed material

The director gives students outlines, worksheets or other written materials about the music being performed. Student study guides can include information about musical structure, forms, historical styles, arranging, and many other important topics. Adjudication check sheets and other evaluative tools can be used, also. Several outlines and student study sheets are presented as illustrations in later chapters. Such materials provide handy sources of information for students. Another advantage is that students can study these materials on their own time.

Ease of administration is one advantage of this approach. However, several questions will arise: Do students understand the material? How well do they understand? Did they *in fact* study the material? It would seem that some type of follow-up is necessary. Evaluation could proceed from an informal discussion to a written test.

Again, no change in rehearsal routine is needed for this type of presentation unless a follow-up is used. Rehearsal time would be necessary for this. Allocate five minutes within several rehearsals for discussion or a longer part of one rehearsal for testing.

Prepare program notes

The director prepares and provides extensive program notes for concert music. If concerts are an outgrowth of rehearsals, what more logical way could be found for presenting information about the music being studied? The approach is somewhat limited, yet very effective if the programming includes many styles. Many conductor's scores now provide adequate program notes. To be of value for teaching musicianship, however, the program notes must concentrate upon the structural, stylistic aspects and not the typical, nonmusical, poetic considerations.

Program notes also make the concert more enjoyable for the audience. The comprehensive notes used for study may have to be trimmed and simplified, however.

Many directors present their program notes orally to the audience. A knack for good public speaking and cool control of "conductor's nerves" would seem to be minimal prerequisites for this. I still remember my high school conductor explaining our music to the audience. He was good at it and how I looked forward to concerts because of it. I wished that he had done more of it for us in rehearsal.

The learning experience can be improved for students if program notes are the result of student research and if they are discussed in class. No extra rehearsal time is needed, unless class time is used for discussion of the information included in the program notes.

Assign out-of-class study

Daily assignments have long been utilized by top band directors. These assignments usually emphasize individual technical improvement. Yet, they need not be limited to technique. Examples of other types of assignments include record listening, selected readings, theory exercises, research and written reports of research.

Record listening should be directed toward the music being

performed. Tone quality can be imitated, stylistic interpretation noted and emulated, and technical and rhythmic problems analyzed. Students can follow the score for the "big picture." If transcriptions are used, the original version should also be studied.

Outside readings should include relevant background materials about music being played. Students can read about historical periods, compositions, composers, forms and structural elements.

Theory assignments should emphasize the relationship of structure to performance. For example, "What are the types of cadences and how do they function in phrases you play?"

Student research should be directed to problems about music being performed. It was suggested earlier that students prepare program notes. In general, give students a topic or problem and "turn them loose" on it.

The out-of-class assignment approach does not take up rehearsal time. As most of the previous plans, however, this procedure would be most effective combined with class discussion.

Utilize class discussion

The director uses lecture, discussion, and demonstration to present important concepts. The band functions as a seminar or laboratory group for learning. This plan is advocated for its total efficiency, especially if used with other procedures. Long dry lectures are not recommended. Instead, demonstrate forms and styles, and portray structural concepts for students. Use audio-visual materials, mimeographed materials, and out-of-class assignments. Rehearsal time is also needed, so rehearsal routines must be constructed to accommodate the type of presentation desired. Two rehearsal routines may be used:

1. The director may take several minutes of rehearsal time as needed. Band literature is carefully chosen for the illustration of concepts. Lecture and discussion is incorporated into the rehearsal. Learning materials are prepared and distributed. Careful attention is paid to consistency and continuity of presentation. In general, the curriculum as outlined in Chapters 2 through 14 is followed extensively, and careful evaluation of progress is made. The works are programmed on a concert.

2. The director may take one or more complete rehearsals for

presentations, demonstrations, lecture and discussion. The "musicianship" rehearsal consists of the performance of the music that specifically illustrates the concepts to be learned. Difficult music can be rehearsed prior to the "lesson" day. Learning materials and outlines are used also. The work is programmed on a concert.

The "Bernstein" approach can be used effectively here. For example, to learn about thematic development, (1) important themes are located, (2) students play them, and (3) students listen to what happens to them throughout the composition. This is a good introduction to the study of form, especially if study outlines are provided.

Provide music subject electives

The school may offer additional courses outside of regular rehearsal time. Strictly speaking, this is not a rehearsal method but is included for completeness. Many large school systems offer courses in music theory, music history, and music appreciation. These courses seem to provide the best opportunity for teaching musicianship in an academic setting through concentrated listening and writing of exercises. Thus, "musicianship" can be taught as it is in college. Unfortunately, the typical college problems may also accrue—compartmentalization and abstraction. What is the relationship of theory to practice (performance)? The added course loses the unique laboratory situation of the full rehearsal with the active participation of the performing musicians. It further limits total student participation because of scheduling and credit problems caused by another special class.

One director uses an alternative plan that resolves this dilemma. His school has modular scheduling which allows for regular sectional rehearsals. When performance is not pressing, he uses this time with the smaller groups to study and discuss style. He utilizes good stereo equipment and exemplary recordings. The learnings are applied and reviewed in the full rehearsal.

Another possible alternative is an informal class that meets before school and receives no credit. I have used this plan successfully in the past to teach conducting to my high school bandsmen. Student interest must be high for it to be successful.

LONG RANGE CONTINUITY

A major strength of the proposed curriculum is that it has "content"—students learn more than performance skills. They learn about music, its theory, styles, and values. By taking a cyclic approach, the learnings can be spread to a three or four year sequence to match the high school structure. A possible three year curriculum consists of the following sequence.

First year:	Timbre and materials of music
Second Year:	Forms and styles of music
Third year:	Interpretation and discrimination of music

In a four-year curriculum "form" and "style" would encompass one year each.

Concentration upon one content area would not result in the complete omission of the other areas. After initial presentation, review is necessary and should be continuous for efficient learning and reinforcement. This cyclic approach is further required by the entrance of new students into the organization each year. With such a curriculum, the administration can no longer accuse the band program of being the same year after year. Students will not only develop in technique but in musicianship as well.

THE CONDUCTOR AS TEACHER

The single, most important factor in the success of a program as advocated here is the band director. He must be excited about his job and enthusiastic for good music well played. Above all, he should think of himself first as a teacher.

Even professional conductors can be considered teachers. According to a study by Ward Woodbury, the professional conductor

> ... is believed to be a teacher by many players in the sense that he gives them, in rehearsal, his interpretation of the composition. The conductor has the advantage of the full score and supposedly a superior knowledge in the whole field of orchestral literature and its interpretation. It is up to him to present his conception to the players through gesture and stimulating instruction. . . .The

degree to which a conductor inspires his musicians to better performances is also indicative of his capacity to teach well.[1]

In a similar vein, Dimitri Mitropolis has said that the conductor must learn the score, analyze it, and know in advance what he wants to express in every phrase. Then he must *teach* it to his musicians, and be able to draw it forth from them in the performance.[2]

However, learning is incidental to the main objective of perfected performance in professional organizations. On the other hand, learning is central to school music groups. The purpose of the professional organization *is* performance; the purpose of the school group is education *through* performance. School rehearsals should be planned to develop musicianship and broad musical understanding of students.

Both the professional and the high school directors must tell their players what to do musically. Often, the high school director must also explain how to do it and, in addition, he should tell them why. For example, the professional conductor may simply ask for *staccato,* but the band director may have to explain and demonstrate the concept of *staccato* as a musical style, and how to achieve this articulation on each different instrument. Furthermore, correcting the school group by using technical terms, even if they are understood by the students, is often not enough for learning purposes. To demand a *crescendo* and *poco accelerando* in a certain passage does not explain why the particular interpretation should be utilized. Students should be led to see how the music builds and drives to an important structural climax. The *why* gets to the content of the music and to musicianship. By concentrating upon content as well as technique, the student learns more than his individual part. He learns music. Learning about music and developing individual musicianship are the most important goals of the high school band program.

CONTENT AND ORGANIZATION OF THE CHAPTERS

Teaching musicianship in the band rehearsal requires similar strategies as teaching musicianship in other music classes. Students

---

[1] Ward Woodbury, "Leadership in Orchestral Conducting," *Journal of Research in Music Education,* Vol. III, No. 2, Fall 1955, p. 127.

[2] Rose Heylbut, "The Making of a Conductor," *Etude,* Vol. LXVII, January, 1954, p. 61.

study timbre, structural elements, forms and styles. The Contemporary Music Project of MENC suggests the following content to foster musicianship.

> The basis for developing more comprehensive musicianship is a "common-elements" approach which views all musics, from all times, as consisting of the same basic musical elements, which might be outlined as follows:
>
> *Sound,* divisible into
>   1. Pitch
>   a. horizontal (melody)
>   b. vertical (harmony)
>   2. Duration (rhythm)
>   3. Quality
>   a. timbre
>   b. dynamics
>   c. texture
>
> These elements are used to articulate shape, or *form.* Every musical work must be viewed in its many contexts—stylistic, historical, cultural, social and economic.[3]

The CMP outline can help the director and his students grasp and synthesize the total content of this book, which has been organized to meet the needs of today's high school band programs.

Chapter 2 investigates the timbre of the band and illustrates how to improve the band's sound. Chapters 3 through 5 tell how to teach the elements of music. These chapters serve as resource material for the study of musical form and style. Chapter 6 explains how to teach the basic forms of music. Students learn formal principles and formal types. Chapters 7 through 10 tell how to teach style to the band. Historical periods are emphasized. Chapter 11 deals with musical expression and Chapter 12 with musical discrimination and value judgment. Chapter 13 illustrates how to evaluate the total program and Chapter 14 tells how to sell the program to administration and students.

---

[3] Robert J. Werner, "Opus 2," *Newsletter Contemporary Music Project,* Vol. I, No. 2, Winter 1970, p. 1.

2

How to Teach Timbre and
Improve Band Sound

Tone is basic. It is literally the substance of music—the "stuff" of which a band is made. It certainly deserves as much attention as the other aspects of performance. Yet, in the busy day to day rehearsal routine, technique tends to be emphasized most. Sometimes this may be necessary, as during football season when each week the show *must* go on. Rehearsal time is consumed with music reading, "cutting the charts," drill, precision, and showmanship. Whatever positive results are obtained, there seems to be a concomitant deterioration of concert band performance standards, especially in the area of tone. Because of the consistent loud playing, abused embouchures and faulty tone production, the week immediately following marching season is appropriate for initial emphasis upon characteristic and expressive tone quality. Many directors use chorales and sustained-style music then for this very purpose. Although the idea is not new, a consistent effort is

27

necessary to effect a long-term upgrading of band sound. In this chapter, specific suggestions are presented for improving the individual tone quality of band members and total band sound through rehearsal procedures, workshops, ensembles, and the study of orchestration.

IMPROVING INDIVIDUAL TONE QUALITY IN REHEARSAL

The first step in improving the sound of the high school band is to improve the tone quality of the individual members within the group. Directors should remember that the unrefined tone quality of only a few members will tend to predominate and destroy an otherwise good ensemble sonority. The following procedure is suggested to promote individual improvement of tone in a group situation. Obviously, this plan could be adopted most effectively for use in sectional rehearsals and individual lessons.

1. The director must bring about an initial awareness of the problem. Students usually just don't know. Slow, sustained, lyrical, and technically easy music is best to initiate tone study. After playing through the composition, carefully select several students to repeat the passage individually or together. (They should exemplify the problem, yet not be overly embarrassed or musically thwarted by the experience. Improvement, after all, is the ultimate goal.) For most students, this type of demonstration is sufficient to portray the problem. The director can illustrate further with the old musical maxim, "The hardest note to play is a whole note." It becomes quite obvious that work needs to be done on tone quality.

2. Next, the student must develop a correct conception of tone for his instrument. Therefore, the director must make available to the bandsmen examples of valid, characteristic and expressive tone quality. There are several possible methods for providing this model tone: (a) The director, himself, can demonstrate the instruments upon which he is capable. (b) Competent, perhaps professional, musicians can play for the students. (c) Students can listen to top-quality, high-fidelity recordings. (d) They can attend symphony orchestra concerts or other professional performances. (e) A student from the band who has the most characteristic tone can demonstrate by performing passages from compositions being rehearsed by the band. Whatever the method, a model tone quality

must be presented to the rank and file student so that he knows exactly what he is to accomplish. He must listen, think and imitate in order to learn.

3. Having heard characteristic tone quality and now having gained a conception, the student must carefully evaluate his own tone—compare it with the conceptual model to determine what improvement is necessary. Go "down the line" for several minutes in the rehearsal to check a section. This can be done in conjunction with hearing individual parts played for rhythmic accuracy or other technical reasons. To save rehearsal time, however, use a tape recorder. Students can singly check their tone by taking turns during regular rehearsal time with the tape recorder in an adjoining room or practice room. They may also use it during free periods or study hall. They give their name, then play and listen. This also provides the director with a record of their initial attempts.

4. The student must now practice intelligently to improve. He must strive to achieve the best tone quality he can, as guided by his conception of a characteristic tone. Slow melodic lines and sustained tones provide the best practice material.

5. As this general cycle of "conception, practice, evaluation" continues, the director must help detect and correct errors and concurrently point up and reinforce improvements.

a. Check breath support, explain it, and offer suggestions. Approach this by "feel." For example, have students hold their waists to feel the expansion all the way around, like an inner tube. Have them lean forward in their chairs to feel the inhalation, and then feel the "support" during exhalation. Next, have them punch with clenched fists as they shout "Hah!" Then, immediately play a tone with this same feeling. Watch that you are not blown off the podium.

b. Check individual embouchures and offer suggestions.[1]

c. Check tonguing for throat constriction and other faults.

d. Check instruments for faulty equipment, especially key mechanisms, mouthpieces and reeds.

---

[1] See Philip Farkas, *The Art of Brass Playing* (Bloomington, Indiana: Brass Publications, 1962) and Everett L. Timm, *The Woodwinds* (Boston: Allyn and Bacon, Inc., 1964).

e. Make further tape recordings and compare these with initial tapes to assess improvement.

f. Have students listen to each other. Hearing and evaluating others fosters individual improvement. Thus, self-evaluation, group evaluation, and teacher-pupil evaluation can be used. Develop a critical but helpful atmosphere.

g. Tape record students on a regular basis to determine improvement. Recordings can be made at the beginning, middle and end of each semester. The tape recorder can be used also in conjunction with the StroboConn to observe pitch control on sustained tones.

h. Use positive reinforcement whenever possible.

TRY A TONE IMPROVEMENT WORKSHOP

The cycle outlined above is suggested for use in rehearsal. Certainly, whatever time is spent on this program will benefit your band. However, if a curtailed rehearsal schedule and concert commitments preclude extensive tone work with your band, a less time-consuming method of initial presentation has been successfully used by the author on several occasions.

The idea originated as an alternative plan for the usual massed band festival, which seems to help no student musically, and the select band clinic, which excludes the poorer players who need the most individual help. The alternate plan took the form of a workshop under the title "How to Get a Good Tone on Your Instrument." All students were included, therefore many clinicians were needed. College specialists were contacted who brought advanced student performers with them. These college students were members of woodwind, brass, and percussion ensembles that performed as part of the workshop. Several high school band directors who were outstanding instrumental performers completed the "staff." Thus, at least one specialist on each band instrument was engaged to present a master lesson on tone quality. Students were divided into groups of like instruments, and the larger "like groups" were later subdivided by ability for individual help after the master lesson, e.g., first, second, and third clarinets.

In general, the day's activities followed this format: (1) After arrival, students went to assigned classrooms for the master lesson. The master teacher demonstrated, lectured, and provided materials for the students concerning embouchure, breath support, tonguing, fingering, reeds, and equipment. Students were required to bring pencil and paper to take notes. (2) After the demonstration period every student, in turn, played a short passage that he had prepared for the clinician who checked for correct embouchure and breath support, adequate equipment, and general tone characteristics. Clinicians offered suggestions and made corrections. During this time, discussion was opened to the group. Thus, observation of others became an important part of learning. (3) After lunch, all students attended an informal concert presented by the college ensemble groups and selected soloists. This provided another opportunity to develop tonal conception. (4) During the final part of the day, clinicians coached high school ensemble groups that were preparing for festival competition. These coaching sessions were also opened for student and faculty observation.

The result of the workshop was instant tone improvement for the eight participating bands. The directors felt that this was the most successful and helpful clinic that they had ever attended. Incidentally, the cost was minimal because only two clinicians received a fee, the others received expenses. On a small scale, even a single band workshop would seem quite feasible—call upon your friends and colleagues, and be prepared to lend your support to their similar undertakings.

IMPROVING SONORITY IN THE BAND

Concurrently with the individual efforts at tone improvement, the director should strive to enhance the total band sound in the full rehearsal. He should explain to students that composers utilize instrumental colors and contrasts for expressive purposes. Since composers either "meld together" or "juxtapose" sounds, blend and balance are important aspects of total band sonority. Careful attention to dynamics as marked in the parts provides the first step. Good intonation is also necessary for clear, "clean" ensemble tone and resonance. Thus, listening at all times must be stressed for correct tone, balance, blend, intonation, and dynamics. The following procedures will help students understand and achieve the desired total band sound.

1. The total band sonority must be balanced. The director is in the best position to balance and blend choirs for a perfect *tutti*

sonority. However, when listening to high school bands, one frequently hears the basic colors out of balance, especially in successive passages of wide dynamic contrast. The group sounds like a "woodwind band" in soft passages and a "brass band" in loud passages. This results because woodwinds tend not to change dynamic levels as markedly as brasses. On the other hand, one also hears the consistently overbalanced brass or percussion sound, or the anemic woodwind-dominated quality of the formerly popular *sotto voce* sound. Although balance in this sense is mostly under the control of the conductor, students should be instructed to listen carefully, especially at lower dynamic levels to achieve correct balance and blend.

2. Soloistic passages and melodic lines should predominate. This refers to the other aspect of balance—juxtaposition or contrast of color. The meaning of balance in this sense can be demonstrated quite easily to the band by having a piano accompanist play his part loudly enough to nearly obscure a soloist. In a similar way, the director can point out a melodic line in the band music that must be projected by the soloist so that it is not covered by the accompaniment. As a general rule, the soloist should play one dynamic degree louder than marked and use a full, rich, "soloistic" tone to project. The accompanying parts must be cautioned to play softly enough to hear the solo line clearly, regardless of their dynamic markings. Accompanying parts should themselves be rehearsed for tone quality as well as rhythmic accuracy. Listen to the sound of just the bass and off-beat parts in any march to confirm this.

3. The woodwind and brass choirs provide the two principal expressive colors of the band. Have the students listen to these basic sonorities by first having the woodwinds, and then brasses play. Decide whether they should be blended or contrasted within a given *tutti* passage. The Vaughan Williams *English Folk Song Suite* offers a good challenge for this exercise, as well as the Gabrielli and Haydn examples presented later in this chapter. Finally, the outstanding *Suites of Carols* by Leroy Anderson feature the woodwind and brass choirs, and provide excellent and diversified program material.

4. The percussion section must also be considered an integral part of the band. The old attitudes that the drums should "just keep

the beat," or "stay with the director," or "be felt but not heard" are clichés of the glorious past. The recent emphasis in contemporary composition illustrates that the percussion section is *the* color and effects "choir" in the band. More diversified training and additional equipment are needed in many schools. Play works for percussion to help bring out their full color potential. The band should be exposed to the wide color effects of percussion in rehearsal.

5. Several subgroups or families further illustrate the color potential of the full band. For example, the woodwind choir is composed of the following basic tone colors: flutes, double reeds, clarinets, and saxophones. These "sub-colors" can be contrasted and demonstrated in rehearsal as they are used by the composer and arranger. Vincent Persichetti's style of composition provides excellent examples of writing for the choirs and subchoirs within the band. Furthermore, his *Divertimento for Band, Psalm for Band, Symphony for Band, Pageant, Ballad for Band,* and *Serenade for Band* rank among the finest literature for winds. The *Serenade* is the easiest. Yet, like the others, it can serve well to illustrate the color potential of subgroups and their contribution to the total band sound. These subdivisions provide the instrumentation for the ensembles discussed in the next section.

THE SMALL ENSEMBLE PROGRAM AND TONE

Outstanding high school band directors have long known the values of an active ensemble program. Chamber playing is the fastest road to musicianship. It develops musical independence, improves sight reading, fosters listening, and generally makes students aware of performance problems such as balance, blend, intonation, precision, and *tone!* An active ensemble program can be developed in which students work primarily on their own time, in their own homes, and for their own enjoyment. All band students should be encouraged to participate in groups and even form their own ensembles. Furthermore, there are numerous possibilities for performance at civic organizations, at school, and at festivals. With this type of motivation, the program can almost run itself, with the director serving as a coach as needed. However, the purpose here is not primarily to justify and promote the ensemble program. It is rather to suggest that chamber groups, ensembles, and instrumental choirs can be used to great advantage to teach the tonal colors of the band *to* the band. Students learn much within the smaller ensemble, and they can also help teach their larger organization. They serve as "conception givers" to illustrate instrumental color.

Ensembles can perform for the band either in rehearsal or at informal programs after school. At these sessions the director should discuss various tonal problems as illustrated in the following examples:

1. How tone is produced
2. Correct conception
3. Embouchure
4. Breath support
5. Balance and blend
6. Effect of intonation upon tone quality
7. The distinctive qualities of the instruments and their contribution to total band color.

ASSISTING STUDENT ARRANGERS

The author knows of several high school groups for which football band arrangements, stage band "charts," and even concert compositions have been written by student members after receiving minimal instructions from the band director.

A band director in one Midwestern high school related how the desire to arrange had become very contagious in his organization after he initially played some student works. His students first arrange for various ensemble groups, and eventually for the full band. Another director commented that arranging was the principal reason that one of his students remained in band despite the academic and parental pressures brought to bear on him. Thus, arranging seems to compete quite favorably with other in-school and out-of-school activities which occupy more and more of the student's time.

To get started, provide your students with an arranging "data sheet" that consists of a listing of band instruments in score order, their practical playing ranges, and their exact interval of transposition. Of course, interested students can compile such a chart themselves from a reference book. For this reason arranging texts should be included in the band library for student use.[2] Manuscript paper and sample full scores should also be made available. In this way, a minimum of the director's valuable time is necessary to initiate individual effort. However, sustained activity and efficient learning require a culminating experience: students must have the opportunity to hear their arrangements performed or, at least, played through. This provides motivation, and pinpoints errors of conception, technique and notation. Tape recording these projects is another effective teaching device. It provides students access to their work for review and learning, and allows the director to make additional comments in private when more time is available.

The final sections of this chapter are devoted to specific projects that the director can use to stimulate interest in arranging, and awareness of timbre to improve band sound.

A PROJECT FOR TEACHING TIMBRE

Several suggestions were made earlier for teaching tone quality in the full rehearsal. The following comparison of two versions of Gabrielli's *Sonata pian'e forte* will serve to illustrate the technique further. The tone color of instrumental choirs and principles of orchestration form the basis of the learning tasks.

Procedure

The director's first step is to prepare the lesson. (1) Study the scores for rehearsal purposes. (2) In addition, analyze the orchestration of both scores. (3) Finally, prepare study materials for band members. See the suggested "Student Study Sheet" in Figure 2-1.

The second step is to rehearse the two versions of the sonata for performance. Ideally, band members should perform both versions in rehearsals and concert. If this is not feasible, the Eastman Wind Ensemble has an excellent recording of the original sonata on Mercury, SR90245. Perhaps some directors may question the

---

[2] Two practical texts for library reference are (1) Philip Lang, *Scoring for the Band* (New York: Mills Music Inc., 1950) and (2) Joseph Wagner, *Band Scoring* (New York: McGraw Hill Book Co. Inc., 1960).

validity of the band transcription. However, the composition certainly has historical significance and musical merit. Furthermore, the transcription serves well for learning purposes.

The third step is to devote one rehearsal to a thorough comparison of the two versions. Use an opaque projector for a visual comparison of the scores. The following points should be brought out in the rehearsal.

1. How the tone color available to the modern arranger is varied and contrasting as compared to the limited color palette of early music.
2. How the color of the composition is altered by the addition of woodwinds and percussion, although the original harmony and musical form are not changed.
3. How the use of more instruments adds "weight" or thicker sonority to the whole.
4. How the increased range afforded by woodwinds adds "breadth" to the composition.
5. What an arranger can do with a fairly simple setting.
6. How the various choirs within a band can "sound." Performance of choirs instead of constant *tuttis* requires careful listening to balance and blend.
7. How dynamic shading marked in the transcription differs in tonal effect from the terrace dynamics of the original.
8. How the written tenuto marks are used by the arranger to illustrate the desired style of tone as well as articulation.

The final step is the actual performance of the work in concert. The contrasting settings make interesting program material. Program notes consisting of a simplified comparison of the two versions of this work have proven to be enjoyable to the audience. The performance also affords an additional review and reinforcement of learning for the band members.

Figure 2-1

STUDENT STUDY SHEET

SONATA PIAN 'E FORTE, from *Sacrae Symphoniae* by Giovanni Gabrielli. Composed in Venice, 1597.

Brass version: Music for Brass No. 45, Robert King Music Company.
Band transcription: arranged by Maurice Gardner, Staff Music Publishing
Company.

Background Information

This composition dates back to the late sixteenth century, when composers
first began assigning specific instruments to the various parts in the score.
Thus, Gabrielli was one of the first practitioners of the art of orchestration.
He was also a very pragmatic musician, utilizing the choir lofts of St. Marks
Cathedral in Venice to enhance his compositions. In its original setting the
Sonata pian 'e forte requires two antiphonal choirs of four instruments each.[3]
Gabrielli specified a cornetto [4] and three sackbutts [5] in the first choir, and
viol and three sackbutts in the second choir. However, in contemporary
performances trumpets and trombones are usually substituted for the original
instruments.

The Gardner arrangement is for full band, and the two choirs of the
original tend to lose their identity. The function of choir I is usually taken by
the woodwind choir, while choir II is generally given to the lower brass as in
the original. Note in the following analysis how the *tutti* band is used, and
how three distinct choirs emerge in addition to the full band—high brass
choir, low brass choir and woodwind choir.

Analysis and Comparison of Instrumental Usage

KING PUBLICATION

mm. 1-14 Choir I: two trumpets
and two trombones. No doubling of
octaves. Lean, thin, concise sonority.

STAFF PUBLICATION

(Choir I) The use of woodwinds
and first horn alters the original
timbre. (Saxes are cued.) Wider
ranges and resulting octave
doubling alter the original sonority
also. The effect is similar to adding
eight and sixteen foot stops to an
organ in four part writing. Dynamic
shadings alter tone and expression.
Note this difference throughout.

---

[3] It is interesting to note that many *avant-garde,* contemporary composers are using
the aisles and balconies of present day concert halls for antiphonal effects.

[4] *Cornettos* are early instruments with cup mouthpieces. However, they utilized tone
holes and key mechanisms like woodwinds to play all notes, not valves.

[5] *Sackbutts* are early trombones.

mm. 14-25 Choir II: three trombones and baritone. The substitution of trombone for the original viol makes balance and blend easier to attain within the choir, but loses the unusual color effect. A viola should be tried if available, and a trombone used instead of baritone to approximate more closely the original color.

(Choir II) Very similar to the King brass version. Lower brasses are used with tuba added at the octave for sonority.

mm. 26-31 Both choirs are utilized within a two octave span. The difference between these two versions at this point can be likened to an arrangement of a "pop" tune for a combo versus an arrangement of the same tune for a big stage band.

Scored for full band, including tympani. This gives a great total impact of sound and a four octave range of instruments. Generally, a thicker sonority and wider breadth of sound than the original.

mm. 31-34 Choir I

(Choir I) Woodwinds, less saxes.

mm. 34-40 Choir II begins, then antiphonal alternations continue at short range.

(Choir II) Lower brasses begin, then alternations with woodwinds (Choir I).

mm. 40-43 Doubled choirs

Full band, with tympani, substitutes for the doubled choirs of the original.

mm. 43-51 Antiphonal writing for Choirs I and II.

Alternation of woodwinds (Choir I) and lower brasses (Choir II).

mm. 52-55 Doubled choirs

Tutti band.

mm. 56-60 Antiphonal writing of Choirs I and II.

The arranger takes several liberties to contrast this section further. At m. 56 the three-part cornets and first trombone take over the function of Choir I. This is similar to the original. However, at m. 58 the woodwinds now play the Choir II part. The color of low register flute and reeds is quite effective, but quite a departure from the original.

mm. 60-63 Alternation of choirs continues.

The full brass section, plus saxophones are scored in this passage. Upper instruments (Choir I) alter-

mm. 63-65 Doubled choirs

mm. 65-68 Short-range antiphonal scoring of the two choirs.

mm. 68-end Doubled choirs except for short antiphonal and imitative passage in mm. 71-72.

nate with lower instruments (Choir II). The effect is much like the original.

Full band, plus tympani.

Another radical departure from the original which illustrates the effective use of choir colors. The arranger through his voicing and use of all the instruments at his disposal, achieves the effect of three choirs in this brief, three-bar passage—Choir I (upper brass), Choir II (lower brass) and "Choir III" (woodwinds).

Tutti style, except for brief antiphonal and imitative passage between low brass (Choir II) and woodwinds (Choir I) in mm. 71-72.

OTHER PROJECTS

A similar approach can be taken comparing an original version of a Classical era band work, *March for the Prince of Wales* by Franz Joseph Haydn, published by Musica Rara, and its modern full band arrangement by James Riley, published by G. Schirmer.

The following points can be brought out in rehearsal concerning instrumentation and orchestration.

1. Difference between original and modern arrangement.
   (a) Key, harmony, and form are the same; only the instrumentation is changed. The original setting calls for Eb trumpet, two Eb horns, two Bb clarinets, two bassoons and serpent.[6]
   (b) Compass of instruments is the same in both with two exceptions. The flute part in the modern version exceeds the range that Haydn used in his setting. Also, the high E b trumpet part is adjusted an octave lower for modern B b trumpets.

---

[6] The serpent is an ancient bass-wind instrument so named because of its resemblance to a large snake. The tone is unrefined and rough. It has been replaced in modern bands by the tuba. Also, drum parts have been added by the editor. Originally drum parts were improvised.

    (c) The primary difference in sound is clarity and sonority. The modern arrangement is thickened in sonority by the scored doubling of instruments and by the addition of instruments and parts standard in today's larger concert bands.

2. Difference between the original Gabrielli and the original Haydn scores.

    (a) Larger span of notes used in the Haydn.

    (b) Greater variety of color available to Haydn.

As with the Gabrielli sonata, the original setting and the modern arrangement of the Haydn march can be used effectively in concert. Both versions can be played in their entirety, or sections can be alternated in the repetitions between the original and modern arrangement. Alternation is accomplished quite easily because of the format of both versions. Furthermore, there are copious program notes provided with the scores. Thus, a concert presentation can feature an interesting demonstration of the evolution of the wind band. If, however, it is not possible to perform both versions, the original setting is available on *Baroque Records,* B 2812, performed by the Wind Ensemble of the Leipzig Academy.

A simpler method of demonstrating arranging techniques and color potential is to play an original Sousa march, followed immediately with a "six way" version of the same work. By listening to and comparing the parts, especially the high woodwinds, the students can see how simplification and editing affects the total sound of the work. The same type of comparison can be made by studying a composition transcribed for band by two different arrangers, as for example, the Leidzen and Walters arrangements of the "Finale" from the *New World Symphony.* This approach offers one additional listening and comparing possibility since the original work is performed and recorded by an orchestra. Listening to the recording should help improve both tone and performance as it gives students further insight into the work itself. It may, at the director's discretion, introduce the bandsmen to the transcription versus original band work controversy, about which so much has been written.

Another work worthy of study is the *Pictures At An Exhibition* by Moussorgsky. This composition was originally written for piano, but is perhaps better known in its orchestral setting by Ravel. The work has also been transcribed for band in a published version by Erik Leidzen and in manuscript by Mark Hindsley. A recording of the Hindsley arrangement is available from the University of Illinois Bands. As an arranging project, one of the shorter movements, such as the "Catacombs" or "Promenade," could be given to a student arranger in its original setting as a piano solo. The student could actually arrange all or part of the movement and then compare his attempt with a published version. This would give the student an immediate on-the-spot comparison of his work with an acknowledged authority on arranging—be it Ravel or Leidzen—without making it necessary for him to be constantly assisted or advised by the busy band director.

3

How to Teach the Musical
Elements: Rhythm

Tone is the substance of music. Rhythm is its duration. Rhythm is the only structural element that can exist independently of the other elements. Both melody and harmony exist in time, hence in a rhythmic framework. The ability to abstract rhythm from its musical context provides a handy teaching device, since rhythm is the most persistent problem in music reading. Band students seem to have much less trouble playing the notes than putting the notes in the right place. Even though rhythmic reading has been at the core of instruction since beginning-band class, the senior high band director must continue advanced rhythmic training and in some cases remedial rhythmic training.

Ask your students to define rhythm. All students seem to know what it means. Rhythm is the "beat," or the different "kinds" of notes, or, perhaps, "4/4 time." These fuzzy concepts provide the starting points.

In a general sense, "rhythm" refers to the organization of movement in time or space. In music, rhythm results when successive tones of like or varying duration are grouped into perceivable time-units. Studying the various levels of time-organization is necessary to understand rhythm. In this chapter, rhythm is examined from beat to pattern. Specific suggestions are made for teaching rhythm in rehearsal.

TEACHING BEAT AND METER

Beat

"Beat" or "count" refers to the steady, underlying pulse of metric music—the felt pulsations. In much of band music this pulse is overt. It is the beat given by the bass drum and the bass line. Any march can serve as an illustration.

However, often the beat is not obvious, but only implied. The music flows along and the beat is subtly felt within the general rhythmic movement. In Example 3-1, the static effect is enhanced by the extended pedal fifth, bagpipe effect.

Ex. 3–1 *Ye Banks and Braes O' Bonnie Doon*
         by Percy Grainger

© Copyright 1949 by G.Schirmer, Inc., Used by permission.

This type of composition must "swing" in its way just as much as music with a strong explicit beat.

Meter

Meter refers to the grouping of beats into recurring patterns by means of accents.

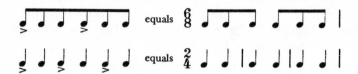

The standard conducting gestures are a visual representation of the meter structure. These conducting patterns evolved with metric music. The first beat of the measure is the strongest. It is represented by a downward motion—the down-beat. The last beat is weak. It is given in an upward direction. The remaining beats are lateral in direction and receive emphasis commensurate with their position in the metric structure.

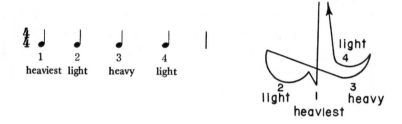

Polymeter

Polymeter refers to the simultaneous use of two meters in different parts. An easily executed example is found in the first movement of Vaughan Williams *Folk Song Suite* at the middle section. The high woodwinds play a *staccato* countermelody in 6/8 above the *marcato* bass melody in 2/4 meter.

Ex. 3–2 *English Folk Song Suite* by Vaughan Williams

A more difficult example occurs in the final movement of Holst's *Second Suite in F* at rehearsal letters C and G. The director must conduct a secure one to a measure while the bandsmen execute the 3/4 against the 6/8 meter.

Ex. 3—3 *Second Suite in F* by Gustav Holst

See also the third movement of Persichetti's *Symphony for Band.*

Uneven Meter

Uneven meter or asymmetrical meter refers to meters of odd-numbered counts as five or seven.

Ex. 3—4 "Mars" from *The Planets* by Gustav Holst, Arranged by G.Smith.

When tempos are fast the asymmetrical meters are often conducted with uneven or "lopsided" beat patterns. This is discussed in the next section.

Changing Meters

In contemporary music, meters often change rapidly to disturb the normal and expected regularity of the beat. The beat or a division of the beat remains constant. Note the effect of the 3/8 measure in Example 3-5. The shift has a syncopating effect in the flow of the music.

Ex. 3–5 "Lord Melbourne" from *Lincolnshire Posey*
by Percy Grainger

The conductor beats out the 3/8 measure at twice the tempo.
The eighth notes remain constant.

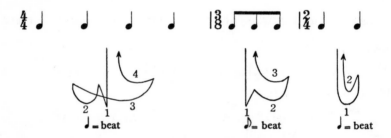

The "Finale" from Breydert's *Suite in F* presents a slightly
different problem. This movement provides an excellent opportunity to teach uneven meter to your group so that they can easily
progress to much more difficult music.

Ex. 3–6 "Finale" from *Suite in F for Band* by Bredert

The instructions in the score indicate that the conductor should use the following counts per measure: 2-1-2-1-2-1-3. The-one-count measures and the three-count measure must be extended in time since eighth-notes must remain equal. This solution is necessary because it is impossible to beat out clearly the three eighth-notes as in the Grainger example. The tempo is too fast. The approach is further clarified if the conductor and bandsmen think eighth-note divisions. The 3/8 measures would have two up-beats. Get your bandsmen to feel the eighth-note pulse by chanting the rhythm together.

Count 2/4 1& 2& | 3/8 1& & | 2/4 1& 2& | 3/8 1& & | 2/4 1& 2&|
Beat   2   1   2   1

Count 3/8 1& & | 9/8 1& & 2& & 3& & |
Beat   1   3

Care must be taken that the measures with "extra" up-beats are not played as triplets. The extra half count must actually be there.

The *Emparata Overture* by Claude T. Smith is handled in a similar way. A rhythmic grouping one measure before letter B results in uneven meter instead of the expected, even execution of 9/8 meter. This measure is grouped

.This is beat in an uneven four and counted "one and two and and three and four and." There are several 7/8 measures in the composition grouped   They are beat in an uneven three and counted "one and and two and three and."

Some conductors prefer to beat out the extra or "added" eighth notes in uneven meter. In this case, the 7/8 example would be conducted with a four pattern and counted "one and two three and four and."

Other examples of uneven and changing meters for band can be found in *Miniature Set For Band* by Donald White (Shawnee), and *Carmina Burana* by Karl Orff, arranged by Krance (Schott).

Nonmetric music

Music that does not have a steady or recurring beat emphasis is called "nonmetric" or "unmetric." Changing meters, uneven meters and displaced accents are contemporary devices that give the effect of nonmetric music, although strictly speaking they are still metric. Solo cadenzas probably provide the best examples of nonmetric music in the instrumental repertory. The performer plays it as he feels it—*ad libitum*. Of course, relative note values and certain traditions help guide the interpretation.

In Example 3-7, the director conducts the flow as he thinks it should move by means of successive down-beats. There is no meter and there are no bar lines.

Ex. 3–7 "Lord Melbourne" from *Lincolnshire Posey*
by Percy Grainger

© Copyright 1940 by G.Schirmer. Used by permission.

READING AND INTERPRETING RHYTHMS

Generally, problems of reading and interpreting rhythms fall into one or more of the following categories: (1) feeling beat units, (2) counting divisions and subdivisions of beat units, (3) achieving rhythmic flow, and (4) achieving evenness of runs and technical passages. Each of these problems is discussed and suggestions are given to help students correct rhythmic deficiencies.

Feeling beat units

Whatever else we know about rhythm, it is a felt, bodily process. Students must feel it to get it. Feeling the basic pulse is the rhythmic fundamental, yet many bandsmen cannot do this.

Marching certainly contributes to this feel for beat. I have students count rhythms and meters while walking from class to class to help remedy rhythmic deficiencies. Any of the elementary school rhythmic techniques that can be applied to the rehearsal are helpful. Clapping the beat, swinging the beat, chanting the beat, or tapping the beat are effective at any level.

Conducting is a good method for helping advanced players gain a bodily feel for beat and meter. Besides giving the beat, the standard conducting patterns are visual representations of meter. Thus, the act of conducting portrays the concepts of beat and meter well. I taught conducting at every high school where I was band director. Classes were always held outside of regular school hours. Yet, they were always well attended and successful. Students came to these noncredit sessions because they enjoyed them. The classes always culminated with actual conducting experiences with the band. Conducting classes in the high school have many values. (1) Students gain a feel for beat and meter. (2) Students learn exactly what conducting gestures mean. Therefore, they follow better. (3) Section leaders are especially attracted to the class. When section leaders become the best followers, the whole group follows better. (4) Conducting students can take over in an emergency. This helps eliminate wasted rehearsal time. The best among them can conduct at school assemblies, pep rallies and concerts.

Counting divisions and subdivisions of the beat

The primary aim of all systems of counting is to provide a method for dividing and subdividing the beat. Note values, after all, do not indicate a fixed length of tone but denote time duration as related to the meter signature, beat, and tempo of the music. For example, the following note symbols, ♩. ♩. ♪ have different lengths as related to meter (3/4 or 6/8), beat value ♩ or ♩. or ♪ and tempo *(allegro* or *adagio).* Similarly "rests" are symbols of the duration of silence as related to the meter, beat and tempo.[1]

The "foot-tap" method with its concomitant down-up (down-beat and up-beat) feel is most consistently used by directors and

---

[1] Rests often require more emphasis in teaching than rhythms. Bandsmen do not learn to count them. Use Grover C. Yaus, *101 Rhythmic Rest Patterns* (Belwin).

advocated in technique books and method books. Of course, the use of foot-beating is reserved for individual practice. There can be only one "giver-of-the-beat" in rehearsal and in concert—the conductor. Yet, the mental image of the downward and upward motion and the internalized feel for it is an important teaching goal.[2] A student study guide like Figure 3-1 is helpful.

Figure 3-1

STUDENT STUDY SHEET

The "Down-up" Feel and Rhythmic Reading

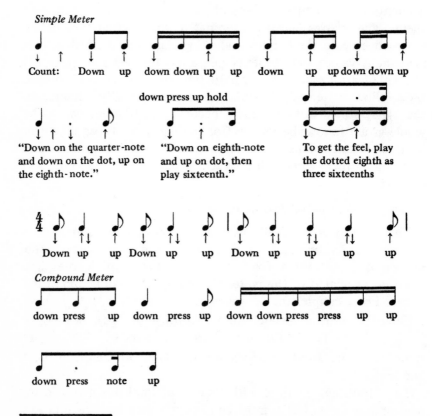

_____

[2] A very complete account of this and other methods of teaching rhythms can be found in an excellent symposium in the *Instrumentalist Magazine*, XXIII, No. 2, September, 1968, pp. 59-76.

The "foot-tap, down-up" system has certain advantages. It fosters a feel for the beat and beat division. It can be taught in a large group situation with relative ease. The weakness is most evident in compound time, where the "Up and down" are no longer even. This often causes confusion and can be deleted.

The next step is to provide students with an outline like Figure 3-2. Have them internalize by "intellect" and by "feel" the four basic concepts of rhythm.

Figure 3-2

STUDENT STUDY SHEET

The Four Basic Concepts of Rhythm

1. *Unit* refers to the kind of note that receives one count.
2. *Simple Meter* refers to the count and its division into twos.
3. *Compound Meter* refers to the count and its division into threes.
4. The *dot* increases the value of a note by one-half.

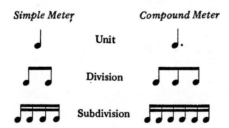

The student counts units, divisions and subdivisions by any system the conductor prefers. For example, in simple time, units could be counted "one two three" etc.; divisions, "one and two and" etc.; subdivisions, "one-a-and-a two-a-and-a," etc. McHose and Tibbs [3] present a complete course of study using rhythmic *solfeggio*. The student conducts the meter (unit) while tapping the division and reciting the rhythm.

---

[3] Allen Irvine McHose and Ruth Northup Tibbs, *Sight Singing Manual*, Third Edition (New York: Appleton-Century-Crofts, Inc., 1957).

Another excellent system has been developed by Larry Teal.[4] In this approach, the subdivisions rather than the divisions are felt by clapping or tapping, and the rhythm patterns are built upon this framework.

Achieving rhythmic flow

Rhythm is the way music moves. Have the student ask himself, "Where is the music going? Where does it lead?" Generally, less important notes receive less emphasis and lead to more important notes. Fast, technical music is easier to perform when students can locate the points for which to aim. In Example 3-8, the line moves up melodically to tonic.

Ex. 3—8 *Egmont Overture* by Beethoven

The eighth-note motive should contribute to the total drive toward the final note. However, students tend to destroy this drive by playing:

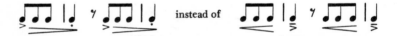

Each group should be slightly intensified to lead inexorably to the top. Emphasis must be placed upon the final note of the group. Long sequences of this motive occur throughout the overture to produce intensity and drive. A scaled extension occurs, leading into the development section.

Ex. 3—9 *Egmont Overture* by Beethoven

---

[4] Larry Teal, *Studies in Time Division* (Ann Arbor, Michigan: University Music Press, 1955).

The first note of the pattern must be exactly on the up-beat of two, even though it is not to be accented. Students have a tendency to be late after rests as well as to accent incorrectly. Finally, the eighth-notes must be played evenly.

The idea of "leading motion" can also help solve the persistent dotted eighth and sixteenth problem. Students tend to group the rhythm the way notes are stemmed, often incorrectly emphasizing the sixteenth-notes. This causes a triplet feel or even results in a space between each written group.

However, a reverse feeling must be taught. The sixteenths lead into the following notes.

The emphasis is upon the long note. The feel for this leading quality can be explained by using the words: "long so-long so-long," or "day to-day to-day."

If the style is *staccato* the separation occurs primarily between the dotted eighth and the following sixteenth. Many directors tell their players to make the dot into a sixteenth rest to help accomplish the correct feeling.

Ex. 3—10 "March" from *Folk Song Suite*
by Vaughan Williams

© Copyright 1924 by Boosey & Company, Ltd. Renewed 1951
Used by permission of Boosey & Hawkes Inc.

Another approach is to delete the sixteenth completely at first and later put it in as a light "grace note."

Even in slow works where the dotted eighth and sixteenth are more connected or slurred together ♪. the sixteenth must retain its feeling of leading into the next note.

Ex. 3–11 "Largo" from *New World Symphony*
by Dvorak

Off-beats can be played more accurately if the forward movement is felt. Have students think "one and two and one and two," instead of "one and two and."

The "leading quality" moves the rhythm with the proper progressive feel.

Phrases are rhythmic units in the flow of music at a larger structural level. A phrase has a large structural "up-beat" and "down-beat." [5] It is initiated and it moves to cadence.

Ex. 3–12 "Song Without Words" from *Second Suite*
by Gustav Holst

phrase up-beat   phrase down-beat

---

[5] See Edward T. Cone, *Musical Form and Musical Performance* (New York: W.W. Norton and Company, Inc., 1968), pp. 25-27.

Achieving evenness of runs

The director must constantly demand that his students think and play technical passages and runs evenly. Lack of skill may be part of the problem. Only unison drill and individual practice can improve technical facility. However, perceptual slips and late responses also cause unevenness and can be corrected by good teaching. The following points should help students.

1. Don't stop at a bar line.

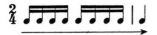

A barline is not a rest or breaking point in the beat or rhythmic flow. It is simply an indication of the metric unit that provides an indispensible guide to the performer. The feeling of movement should always be across the barline to the following down-beat emphasis.

2. Don't stop after a rhythmic grouping.

Remember that notes are grouped by *beat* and not by *movement*.

3. Don't hang on to the first note of a group even though it may be emphasized for metric security.

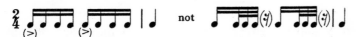

4. Don't be late starting after a rest.

(uneven and/or rushed)

Students tend to make late entrances, then rush through a run. The attack must be exactly on the up-beat. A late start always results in an uneven run.

5. Always think divisions and subdivisions carefully.

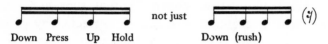

Down   Press   Up   Hold   Down (rush)

6. Practice all technical passages and runs with a metronome to work for absolute evenness.
7. Listen and watch carefully in rehearsal to match rhythms to the conductor's beat.

TEACHING RHYTHMS IN REHEARSAL

Rhythmic teaching will never proceed past rote drill if the director spends all of his time counting out, clapping, or otherwise demonstrating all difficult rhythms for his groups. Independent sight reading ability should be a major aim of the band program. If bandsmen cannot read rhythms, they remain completely dependent upon a teacher during their school career, and become potential drop-outs as post-school players.

To be completely effective, the systems of sight reading and rhythmic counting previously mentioned must be taught to individuals or small groups in a consistent manner outside of full rehearsal. In the high school this amounts to remedial rhythmic training. Yet, much can be done in the full rehearsal to teach rhythmic reading by augmenting the rote approach. The attack must be two-fold: (1) sight reading experience and (2) demonstration, analysis and drill.

Sight reading experience

If at all possible, sight read each new composition through completely. This helps develop a sight reading attitude in your bandsmen. You can use the sight reading procedure of the state music festivals. It provides valuable practice for all bands who participate in festivals. Obviously, a complete read-through is impossible if the music is technically and rhythmically too difficult. However, as the old saying goes, "bands learn to sight read by sight reading."

The read-through also allows the director to listen for the major problems to be corrected in subsequent rehearsals. Wrong rhythms, wrong notes and incorrect style provide the obvious, initial work in rehearsal.

Demonstration, analysis and drill experience

Many directors use drill books to present and teach rhythms to their groups. Ensemble drill books are designed to build musicianship. They attempt to put all "necessary" rhythms between two covers so that students can learn them systematically. However, only you, the director, can select rhythms appropriate for your group and help students learn them by relating them to the music being played. Drill books can help in this process when used in the above manner. Merely assigning each rhythm in the order in which it appears in the book does not relate the drill to the music being rehearsed. There are plenty of rhythm patterns to take from the music. The following examples provide excellent rehearsal problems in rhythm. The rehearsal suggestions can be used after the initial sight reading experience.

Ex. 3—13 "Song of the Blacksmith" from *Second Suite* by Gustav Holst.

© Copyright 1922 by Boosey & Company, Ltd. Renewed 1949
Used by permission of Boosey & Hawkes, Inc.

1. Write the rhythm on the chalkboard. Have all students count and clap it. Then drill the rhythm in unison on the tonic (d minor), very slowly in strict meter. Gradually increase the tempo.
2. Count off every other player in each section. Have half of the group play the unison drill, while the others count for them. Then, reverse the playing and counting roles. (This works well with beginners and intermediates also. Half of the students play while the others count and *point* to the notes as they are played. The director can quickly ascertain who is really reading the music.) After the unison drill, have those bandsmen with rests in their parts, in this case the woodwinds, count for those who have notes to play.

3. Have each section play the unison drill. Listen for those individuals who need special help.

4. Reproduce all of the difficult rhythm patterns and distribute them to the group to practice as a homework assignment.

It may be best to make this particular assignment after class drill. However, assignments can be made prior to rehearsal to allow students to prepare individually. Assignments can also be made from ensemble drill books that contain appropriate rhythm patterns.

5. Play a recording of the work. The Eastman Wind Ensemble has an excellent recording of both Holst *Suites* on Mercury (MG 50088). Much of the standard band repertory is now available on records.[6] I have used recordings of seemingly difficult works that students did not comprehend, did not like, and consequently would not play. Most problems of teaching, including rhythm, were solved almost immediately when students exclaimed, "Gee that's good! I didn't realize it was supposed to sound like that!"

For some reason, many directors do not want to use records for teaching purposes. Good recordings provide the best possible model for tone, interpretation and *rhythm.* If rote learning is the reason not to use recordings—wait until all sight reading and analysis are completed. Then, use the recording as "frosting on the cake" to illuminate the subtle rhythmic emphases and appropriate accentuations that make such a difference in a "polished" performance.

The dotted rhythm in Example 3-10 illustrates the type of "stress-feel" to which I refer. Leaving out the dot results in better articulation. However, it is more difficult to achieve the right

---

[6] See *Band Record Guide* (Evanston, Illinois: The Instrumentalist Co., 1969).

stress upon the dotted eighth-note, and the correct rhythm and leading quality of the sixteenth-note. Students often need the correct aural conception that a model recording provides.

4

How to Teach the Musical
Elements: Melody
and Theme

Ask your students to define the term "melody." Everyone seems to know what it means—it's the "tune" or "song." Students can rarely give a real definition. Next, have your students think about a specific composition, and then try to describe it to the group. The melody or theme is usually the most identifiable feature. It's what we "sing" to ourselves when we "think" of a composition. In a very real sense, the melody—or, more correctly, the theme—is what a composition is all about.

But what exactly is a melody, and how can the concept of melody be presented for students to learn? Simply stated, a melody is a meaningful pattern of notes. It consists of a succession of tones of varying pitch and duration perceived as a configuration (a pattern in its totality). It is interesting to note that Gestalt psychologists used melody as one verification of their theory. They explained that melody is not perceived as a series of individual, separate notes but as a complete entity. "The whole is more than the sum of its parts." Transposition of a melody— moving it from one key to another—does not change the configuration. Although completely different notes may be used in the transposed version, the "tune" remains recognizable because the exact organization or pattern is unchanged. It is this organization or pattern that must be studied to fully comprehend melody. The following organizational components of melody will be brought out in music being performed: tonality, scale, motive, sequence, chromatic structure, serial structure and thematic usage.

TONALITY

Tonality refers to the structuring of melody in a key. Almost any composition you are performing can serve as an illustration. However, familiar tunes like the *National Anthem* make the best examples since many bandsmen do not play the melodic lines. Have students notice that one note dominates the musical organization. The melody, after moving to other pitches, tends to "come to rest" upon this note, and ultimately ends upon it. This dominating note is called the "tonic" or key note. The tonic is the first note of the scale. Thus, to study tonality is to study keys. Tonal melody will always be organized in a key with the keynote or tonic controlling and dominating the organization.

Ex. 4—1 *National Anthem*

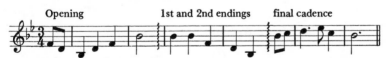

The opening few notes of the *National Anthem* establish the key by outlining the tonic chord. The first section ends on the tonic. The final melodic tone is the tonic.

Ex. 4—2 *Little Fugue in G Minor* by Bach

Bach's *Little Fugue in G Minor* also begins on the tonic chord. Although the theme modulates to several keys, the composition ends melodically on the tonic.

Ex. 4–3 *Ye Banks & Braes O' Bonnie Doon*
by Percy Grainger

In Example 4-3 the dominant pick-up note leads into the tonic to help establish the key at the outset. The second and final phrases of the melody cadence on the tonic.

Studying tonality should help develop key consciousness and key feeling in students. Practicing the transposition of melodies by ear and studying scales will aid in this development. Scale practice should always be related to key feeling and to the music being played.

SCALES

The term "scale" refers to the consecutive placement of all seven different notes of the key (tonality) within an octave. This forms a whole and half-step pattern (Gestalt) that is consistent in all keys.

Ex. 4–4 The Major & Minor Scale Patterns

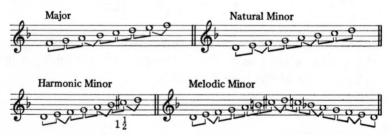

For a good work-out, have your band practice Beethoven's *Prelude Through All Major Keys*, (arr. Erickson, pub. Belwin). Ensemble drill books contain the principal major and minor keys. These can be practiced in conjunction with music being performed. [1]

---

[1] See Leonard Smith, *Treasury of Scales* (Belwin) Fussell, *Ensemble Drill* (Schmitt, Hall and McCreary) and McLeod and Staska, *Scale Etudes* (Schmitt, Hall and McCreary).

Student projects

The most effective method to practice scales on any given instrument is not practical for group study. The full range of the instrument should be covered. Have students play from the lowest possible *tonic* up to the highest possible *note* in the key, then to the lowest possible *note* in the key and finally back to the lowest *tonic*. In this way, the student learns all of the possible (or, at least, attainable) notes of the key on his instrument and a total key-feeling is established.

Have students "abstract" the different notes from music they are playing and place them in scale order. The tonic is the key note and first note of the scale. All tonal melodies are based upon scales. For example, have them play a descending major scale and ask, "What song is this?" Then have them use the rhythm

The key signature indicates the tonic and scale upon which the composition is based. Assign the scale from each work the band is playing. A melody may "modulate" at some point. This simply means it is based upon another scale (key) for that section. Have students practice scales for all modulating sections.

Rehearsal procedures

The following sample lessons illustrate how scales and scale study can be related to music being performed.

Ex. 4–5 *Second Suite* by Gustav Holst.

The opening measures are quite difficult to execute cleanly. As if the crisp *staccato* were not enough of a problem, the unison run of the first measure is awkward and pitched low for the bass instruments. The effect is "muddy" and lacks precision since the instruments do not want to speak when entering "cold." The high woodwinds echo the pattern in the second measure. The *staccato* is difficult and intonation is usually a problem on high "C." The melody begins in measure three on the same five-note run that proceeds up to the octave in measure four. Here then is an ideal place to study and apply the concert F major scale.

The opening run consists of the first five notes of the F major scale. This is repeated by the high woodwinds and repeated once more in the melody, measure three. Then the melody continues up the F major scale. Furthermore, all of the runs throughout this movement are based upon ascending or descending F scale passages.

The F major scale should be practiced in unison, evenly, and slowly at first. Use note values of halves, quarters and finally eights in *alla breve* meter. Then use the following drills that have been taken from the music itself.

1. Everyone play together the first five notes of the scale in the octave that they appear in the parts of the opening measures of the music. Work for strict tempo, evenness of rhythm and clean articulation.
2. Work the slurred woodwind five-note runs which are based upon the opening theme at letter B.
3. Work the descending scale-wise bass runs after A, after C, and before F. Again, unison drill can be used effectively.
4. Assign exercises based on the F major scale from ensemble drill books. These can be especially helpful at the outset since they are in the transposed key for each instrument.

Ex. 4—6 *Prelude & Fugue in D Minor* by Bach

This composition is in the relative minor of F major. The difficulty is to play the ascending melodic-minor scale evenly, accurately and in tune. The melodic-minor scale should be practiced in unison by all students. A drill book can be used for this. However, two scale-wise figures will not be found in the drill books. They must be practiced from the music.

Ex. 4—7 *Prelude & Fugue in D Minor* by Bach

The scale descends and ascends from dominant to dominant, instead of tonic to tonic. Also, the sixth and seventh scale degrees are raised in the descending line. Watch the sharp 1-2-3 valve combinations in the brass and the clarinet throat tones.

Finally, you may wish to discuss scale tendencies with your group. In the tonal system some scale notes are "rest" tones while others are "stress" tones. They have passive or active tendencies in the tonal scheme. This can be illustrated by having students stop on the second to last note of a melody, and noting the tendency or stress to resolution. Use the piano for further demonstration and ear training. Here are the general tendencies of scale tones.

Ex. 4—8

Seventh pulls up to tonic.
Second moves down to tonic or sometimes up to third.
Fourth pulls down to third.
Sixth moves down to fifth or sometimes up to seventh.
Teach students to feel these expressive pulls for interpretation.

In summary, it is most important for the director to relate tonality—the study of keys and scales—to the music being played. Students must understand the importance of this study for their everyday music making. Stress relationship and applicability. After all, the first step toward good intonation is playing in the right key.

MOTIVE

The smallest thematic building block is a motive. Two or more notes are used as a melodic-rhythmic germ from which phrases and melodies are built. Motivic repetition helps give unity and coherence to music. Probably the best known motive illustrating symphonic development is found in the first movement of Beethoven's *Fifth Symphony*.

Ex. 4—9

However, you can find unifying motives in almost any composition you perform. Play the following illustrations and have your students locate the important motives. "Largo" from the *New World Symphony*, Dvorak ♪ ♪ *St. Anthony Chorale*, Haydn ♪. ♪♪♪ "Larghetto" from *Military Symphony in F*, Gossec ♪ ♪ "Trio" from *Stars and Stripes Forever*, Sousa ♩ ♩ ♩

SEQUENCE

"Sequence" refers to the repetition of motives on different, usually successive, scale degrees. Sequences may move either up or down. Most music you play will contain sequence. The *St. Anthony Chorale* by Haydn illustrates both the ascending and descending sequential treatment of the principal motive.

Ex. 4—10 mm. 11—18

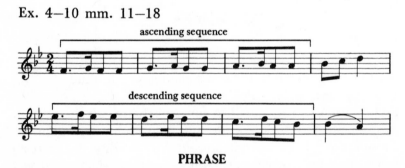

PHRASE

A phrase is a short melodic segment that is complete in itself. As in grammar, phrase refers to a meaningful unit. A phrase ends with a melodic cadence. A "melodic cadence" is a resting place or stopping point in the melody where the onward motion of the music is temporarily interrupted. The cadence may be complete (conclusive, terminal or final), or incomplete (inconclusive, non-terminal or nonfinal).

Ex. 4–11 "Song Without Words" from *Second Suite*
       by Gustav Holst

In performance, have students locate cadences and move the music through to them for expressive phrasing. In this sense, the cadence is not only the ending point of a phrase but also its musical goal. Along the way to cadence, have students look for the phrase climax. Intensity is built to the climactic point and released at the cadence.

Ex. 4–12 "Intermezzo" from *English Folk Song Suite*
       by Vaughan Williams

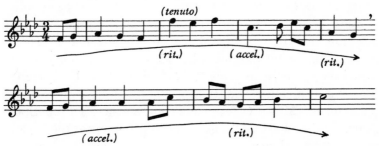

Each phrase is a music unit that is one part of the complete melody, or conversely, melodies are built from groups of phrases.

DIATONIC STRUCTURE AND MELODIC DESIGN

A diatonic melody is a melody based upon a major or minor scale. All of the examples previously quoted have been diatonic. The tonal structure has helped give the melody unity and coherence. Other structural principles work in a complete melody—repetition and contrast of tonal materials. "Repetition" of a phrase or section gives unity to music. "Contrast," that is, introducing a new and different phrase or section, gives variety and interest to music.

Play Example 4-13. Have students listen to what is similar and what is different.

Ex. 4–13 "Largo" from *New World Symphony*
    by Dvorak

Note the incompleteness of measure two that seems to require the repetition in measures three and four, and a more satisfactory conclusion. The first is an "antecedent" phrase that leads to the second, "consequent" phrase. (The form is a parallel period which is discussed further in Chapter 6.) New thematic material is introduced at measure five, that moves to an incomplete cadence in measure six. Measures seven and eight are an exact repetition of measures five and six. Measures nine and ten repeat the beginning two measures. However, measures eleven and twelve are an intensification of measures three and four, ending upon a complete cadence, after first reaching the climax of the melody. The twelfth measure is repeated softly (measure thirteen) and then repeated in augmentation (measures fourteen and fifteen). This extends and rounds off the resolution. The design of the melody is *a a' b b a a''* or more simply *A B A*. Here we have the classic use of musical repetition and contrast: statement-departure-restatement.

Have students analyze these and other melodies for design (melodic form), by locating similar and contrasting phrases.

St. Anthony Chorale, Haydn

"Larghetto" from *Military Symphony in F,* Gossec

"Intermezzo" from *Folk Song Suite,* Vaughan Williams

"Song Without Words" from *Second Suite in F,* Holst

CHROMATIC MELODY

Composers have used the chromatic scale as a basis for organizing melody.

Ex. 4–14 "Mars" from *The Planets*
by Gustav Holst, arr. G.Smith

© Copyright 1924 by Boosey & Company, Ltd. Renewed 1951
Used by permission of Boosey & Hawkes, Inc.

Ex. 4–15 *Rienzi Overture* by Wagner

Although tonal in conception, Wagner was breaking away from the traditional key relationships that had dominated music since the time of Bach. The use of chromaticism eventually led to the serial organization discussed next.

SERIAL MELODY

Serial technique is a contemporary method of musical composition invented by Arnold Schoenberg. He called it the system of composition with the twelve tones related only to one another. Using this method, the composer chooses an arbitrary but calculated arrangement of the twelve tones of the chromatic scale called a "tone row." This series forms the basis of the composition, replacing the traditional tonal system. There is no tonic or no scale upon which the melody is based. Instead, the melody is formed from one of four possible versions of the row—the original, retrograde (backwards), inversion (upside-down), or retrograde-inversion (backwards and upside-down)—which can be transposed to any pitch level or octave by the composer.

There are several serial compositions available to the band, most of which contain complete analyses:

> *Somersault,* Hale Smith (Frank)
> *Three Miniatures for Band,* Frank Erickson (Chappell)
> *Dodecaphonic Set,* William Latham (Barnhouse)
> *Meditation,* Gunther Schuller (Associated)
> *Dirge for Band,* Robert Starer (Leeds)

The Smith composition offers some long, beautiful, lyric lines that are contrasted by rhythmic punctuations in a somewhat jazzy feel. The *Three Miniatures* are more stark but "cute." The final movement is particularly appropriate for illustrating contemporary melody. There isn't too much of what we traditionally call "melody." Instead, short fragments or even single notes are tossed about from instrument to instrument in a pointalistic texture.

Ex. 4–16 *Three Miniatures for Band* by Erickson
© Copyright 1968 by Chappell & Company, Inc. Used by permission.

THEME

When a melody is used as a major unifying and expressive force throughout an extended composition it is called a theme. A theme unifies because it keeps returning. It may return in many different ways: complete, fragmented, varied, modulated, inverted, augmented, to name a few. Themes tend to be open-ended. That is, more needs to follow from a theme, as contrasted to a "closed" melody that is complete in itself.

One way to help students understand long and complicated compositions is to teach them the theme or themes upon which it is based. Then have them listen to what happens to the themes in the course of the work.

Ex. 4–17 *Prelude & Fugue in D Minor* by Bach

A fugue is a good illustration because it is monothematic. Students can concentrate upon its one theme. Have your band listen carefully to the subject (fugue theme) as played by the oboes and clarinets. Write it on the board and have the band sing it to get it firmly in mind. Then, have them listen carefully to what happens to it as they perform the work.

See Chapter 6 for a complete analysis of this fugue, and for further illustrations of themes and thematic development.

5

How to Teach the Musical Elements: Harmony and Texture

Band students tend to concentrate exclusively upon the single line that is written in the part they are expected to play. The very nature of their job can preclude chordal listening unless the director brings out the harmonic implications in the music. Fine intonation, balance and blend depend upon this important facet of individual musicianship. It is also the most difficult to develop in the full rehearsal.

Harmony, the vertical dimension of music, evolved in Western culture. It refers to the structuring of simultaneous tones into chords. As with the other musical elements, the development of harmony was no chance process, excluding aleatoric music, of course. Harmonic organization, like melodic organization, is controlled by tonality in most of the band music played today. In addition to tonality, the other structural considerations that must be investigated to understand harmony are cadence, dissonance, consonance, progression, chromatic chord structure, polychordal structure and serial organization.

TONALITY AND CHORD CONSTRUCTION

The "tonic" controls and dominates harmonic organization as well as melodic structure. The final chord of tonal music will almost always be the tonic chord. Often the initial chord is tonic also. As illustrated earlier in the *National Anthem* and the Bach *Little Fugue in G Minor,* the tonic chord is outlined melodically in the opening measure.

Ex. 5—1

a. *National Anthem*   **b.** *Little Fugue in G Minor* by Bach

It is good rehearsal procedure to play the final (or opening) tonic chord to listen, tune and balance. This helps establish the tonality and provides a landmark for student listening throughout the composition.

Have the band build the tonic chord of each tonal work they are rehearsing by playing the first, third and fifth notes of the scale.

Ensemble drill books and other published materials provide handy aids for chord construction, chord playing and listening. Start with the Selmer *Concert Band Warm-ups.* The sheet includes the keys of E flat and B flat major with the transposed scale for each instrument, tonic chord outline, and a I VI IV V⁷ I progression. The Selmer *Scale Studies for Band* contains the scales in all keys with the tonic triad indicated. These are quite inexpensive. The Belwin *Advanced Fun With Fundamentals* includes scales and chords in most major and minor keys. Other ensemble drill books with harmonic analyses and chords are the Hal Leonard *Advanced Band Method;* Smith, Yoder, Bachman

Technique (Kjos); White *Unison Scale, Chords and Rhythm Studies for Band* (Carl Fischer); and Fussel *Ensemble Drill* (Schmitt, Hall and McCreary).

The next step is to illustrate how chords can be built upon any degree of the scale. Note that some chords are major, minor and diminished. The tonic, dominant and subdominant chords are the most important in traditional harmony, particularly for their function in cadential formulas.

CADENCE

Cadence refers to a stopping or pausing in the flow of music. It was mentioned earlier that a phrase ends with a melodic cadence. A phrase also ends with a harmonic cadence. The cadence is the ending point or goal of the musical phrase. Again, as with melodic cadences, harmonic cadences can give a feeling of incompleteness (pausing with more expected to follow), or completeness (more or less final stopping and ending).

There are several common cadences used in traditional music.

1. The "half cadence" is an incomplete or nonterminal cadence ending on the dominant chord (V or V^7).

2. The "authentic cadence" is usually used as a complete or conclusive cadence because it provides a confirming close and resolution. It consists of a dominant seventh chord (V^7) that resolves to the tonic chord (I). When the tonic note is in the melody and the bass, it is called a "perfect authentic cadence." Play the examples to feel the effect of these cadences. Try cutting off at the half cadence and/or after the dominant chord in the authentic cadence. Ask your students how it makes them feel.

The *Irish Tune from County Derry* by Grainger cadences similarly at measure eight and measures fifteen to sixteen. Also see the *St. Anthony Chorale* by Haydn, measure five and measures nine to ten. You can find many more examples in the music your band plays. These two-phrase patterns are examples of period structure,

Ex. 5–2 *Ye Banks & Braes O' Bonnie Doon*
  by Percy Grainger
© Copyright 1949 by G.Schirmer, Inc. Used by permission.

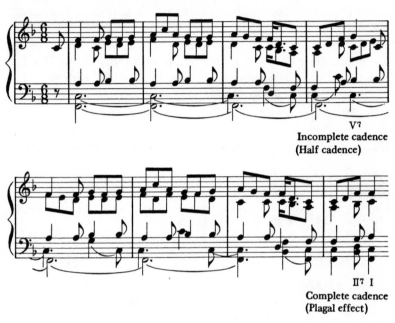

V⁷
Incomplete cadence
(Half cadence)

II⁷ I
Complete cadence
(Plagal effect)

Ex. 5–3 "Second Movement" *Military Symphony in F*
  by Gossec

Larghetto (mm 1-4)

I   V⁷   V⁷   I ————

which will be discussed thoroughly in the next chapter. The following brief summary is given here to clarify cadential usage.

"Period" refers to a grouping of two phrases. The first phrase ends upon an incomplete cadence, usually the half cadence. The harmonic movement is completed by the second phrase which ends upon a conclusive cadence, usually the perfect authentic cadence. Thus, the second phrase completes a harmonic movement left incomplete by the first phrase.

3. The "plagal cadence" is a complete cadence that consists of the subdominant chord (IV) that resolves to the tonic chord (I). The "Amen" at the conclusion of hymns is a plagal cadence. The "Hallelujah Chorus" from the *Messiah* is punctuated throughout with the IV to I progression and ends upon a plagal cadence.

Ex. 5—4 "Hallelujah Chorus" from the *Messiah* by Handel

I   IV   I

4. Some cadences are progressive in function. They move the musical line to new tonal areas. The music modulates to another key. For example the *Egmont Overture* is in the key of F minor. Approaching rehearsal number **5** (in the Winterbottom arrangement) a pedal E flat in the bass begins to establish a dominant E flat chord, which functions as a half cadence one measure before **5**. This leads inexorably to the next section (subordinate theme) in A flat, the relative major of F minor. E flat is the dominant chord of A flat.

Ex. 5—5 *Egmont Overture* by Beethoven

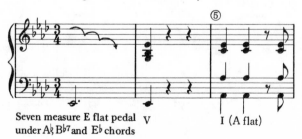

Seven measure E flat pedal V   I (A flat)
under A♭ B♭7 and E♭ chords

DISSONANCE AND CONSONANCE

Reference has been made to active and passive tones in the scale structure. In a similar way, there are active and passive chords in the harmonic scheme. Have the band play a perfect authentic cadence, as for example, from the Gossec "Larghetto" quoted earlier. Hold the V^7 chord to gain the full effect. Wait, and then resolve it to the tonic. Have the students notice that the dominant-seventh chord is unstable and tensional (dissonant). It seems to demand resolution to the stable (consonant) tonic.

Dissonance has been used increasingly in the evolution of music to build intensity and create movement. The usual unpleasant or discordant connotations of dissonance should be replaced in student thinking by the expressive tensional function. In Example 5-6 the harmonic dissonance combined with the melodic, rhythmic and dynamic devices intensify the line toward a recurring statement of a principal theme.

Ex. 5–6 *Psyche & Eros* by Franck (mm. 139–42)

PROGRESSION

Just as the melody moves through intensity points to melodic cadence, chord progressions drive the phrase line through to harmonic cadence. Normal root movement is one important means of harmonic progression, especially by cycles of secondary dominants.

Ex. 5–7 *St. Anthony Chorale* by Haydn (mm 1–5)

Dissonance is another important driving element. Note the minor second dissonances and the effect of the resolution on the B flat major chord.

Ex. 5–8 "Second Movement" from *Three Miniatures for Band* by Erickson (mm 27–28)

© Copyright 1968 by Chappell & Company, Inc. Used by permission.

Chromatic harmony is unstable, often dissonant, tension-producing and moving.

Ex. 5–9 *Rienzi Overture* by Wagner (mm 34–38)

The *Rienzi Excerpts* arranged by Osterling are easier than the overture and contain an excellent example of chromatic harmony in measures 127-47. The music builds through ascending chromatic progression to a climactic resolution on a B flat chord.

CONTEMPORARY HARMONIC TECHNIQUES

Polytonality

Polytonality refers to music written in two or more keys simultaneously. Milhaud's *Suite Française* contains much polytonal writing. Donald White employs the bitonal method of composing throughout his *Miniature Set for Band.* The bitonal analysis is very helpful for rehearsal purposes. Play one progression of triads at a time to balance and tune—first the treble instruments and then those playing the bass clef part. When the parts are put together the total effect will be balanced, tuned and interestingly dissonant.

Ex. 5–10 "Dialogue" from *Miniature Set for Band*
by Donald H.White (mm 19–21)

© Copyright MCMLXIV, Templeton Publishing Company, Inc.

Sole Selling Agent: Shawnee Press, Inc., Delaware Gap, pa. 18327

Serial harmony

Serial technique is a contemporary compositional system which uses the arbitrary but calculated arrangement of the twelve tones of the chromatic scale as the basis for harmony. Traditional harmonic functions are abandoned as the dominant-tonic relationship and conventional root movement. This is replaced by Schoenberg's "twelve tone system." Both melody and harmony are derived from the tone row in one of its forms—original, retrograde, inverted and retrograde-inverted. These rows can be transposed to begin on any of the twelve chromatic steps. The resulting chords are usually quite dissonant and tension-charged.

The harmonic use of the row is explained quite well by Erickson in the program notes for his *Three Miniatures.* The second movement starts with the inverted form of the tone row structured into three-note "chords" that are doubled in the bass clef. Various other harmonic groupings are used throughout this movement.

Ex. 5—11 "Second Movement" from *Three Miniatures for Band* by Erickson

© Copyright 1968 by Chappell & Company, Inc.

Used by permission. (Based upon the Inverted Row)

Latham's *Dodecaphonic Set* begins with loud, rhythmic, tone clusters derived from the original row. Here the row is "stacked-up" vertically. Beginning in the fourth measure the row is stated linearly to form a lyric unison melody. The movement ends as it began with the vertical use of the original row in a rhythmically intensified form.

Somersault by Hale Smith has a very detailed analysis which is included in all the band parts. An excellent lesson plan is included for teaching this serial work to your bandsmen.

Other harmonic devices

Polytonality and serial organization represent but two possible contemporary harmonic treatments. Other modern harmonic techniques include (1) the building up of large chords in thirds, as ninth, eleventh and thirteenth chords; (2) building chords in intervals other than thirds, using fourths or fifths; (3) using modal harmonies based upon ancient scales (modes); (4) using parallel chords; (5) adding tones to chords; (6) ommitting tones from chords; and (7) using tone clusters.

Ex. 5—12

Parallel   added   omitted   tone
chords   tones   tone   cluster

TEXTURE

The term "texture" is used in a special, technical way in music. It refers to the type of voice movement in a composition (to the number of musical lines and the way they are treated by the composer). There are three types of texture—monophonic, homophonic and polyphonic.

Monophonic texture

Monophonic texture refers to a single, unaccompanied melodic line. The texture is extremely rare in band music. Here are several short examples.

Ex. 5–13 *Rienzi Overture* by Wagner (mm 12–19)

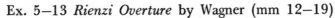

Ex. 5–14 "Fifth Movement" *Dodecaphonic Set*
            by Latham (mm 1–9)

The opening theme statement of Erickson's *Three Miniatures* is monophonic. The "Chaconne" from Holst's *First Suite* begins with a monophonic setting of the theme. The theme of the *Variations on a Korean Folksong* by Chance is first presented in monophonic texture by unison clarinets. The first statement of fugue subjects is monophonic.

Any time a melody is played in unison or octaves with no accompaniment the texture is monophonic.

Homophonic texture

Homophonic texture refers to a melodic line with supporting chordal accompaniment. This texture is very common in band music. Examples include *St. Anthony Chorale* by Haydn, "Song Without Words" from *Second Suite* by Holst, "Intermezzo" from *English Folk Song Suite* by Vaughan Williams and "Largo" from the *New World Symphony* by Dvorak.

Ex. 5–15 "Largo" from *New World Symphony*
        by Dvorak (mm 7–10)

Polyphonic texture

Polyphonic texture refers to two or more melodic lines that move more or less independently, resulting in "counterpoint." Counterpoint literally means "point against point." Musically it means note against note, or line against line. Two types of polyphonic texture are found in band literature.

1. The first type of polyphonic texture results from a compositional technique called "imitation." A theme (or subject) is stated in one voice part. This is answered by the same theme in another voice part in the same key or in a different key. Imitation is used in rounds, canons and fugues.

Ex. 5—16 *Prelude & Fugue in D Minor* by Bach

Tapor by Hovhaness is an excellent example of free imitation. In the passage quoted here short-range imitation (stretto) is also utilized.

Ex. 5—17 *Tapor No.1 for Band*
by Hovhaness (mm 13—14)

© Copyright 1968 by C. F. Peters Corporation, 373 Park Avenue South, New York, 10016. Reprinted with permission of the publisher.

2. Another type of polyphonic texture occurs when two or more different melodies or themes are played simultaneously.

Ex. 5—18 "Trio" from *Stars & Stripes Forever* by Sousa

Holst's *First Suite* begins with a *chaconne.* Here a melody is stated and free variations are written over and against the repeated melody, resulting in polyphonic texture. The "Finale" to the Brahms *Fourth Symphony* (arr. Foote) is another example of the chaconne technique. Variations are written over and around a repeated harmonic pattern. Finally, Jerry Bilik has written an interesting work entitled *American Civil War Fantasy,* in which songs of the Civil War are juxtaposed in polyphonic texture.

The use of several textures in one composition

Composers may utilize all textures within a single composition and often do so to achieve a total expressive effect. Handel composed in the Baroque era, a period of extensive and often exclusive use of polyphonic texture. Have students note Handel's effective use of all textures in his "Hallelujah Chorus."

Ex. 5—19 "Hallelujah Chorus" from the *Messiah*
by Handel

a. Monophonic (mm 12—14)

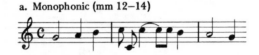

b. Homophonic (mm 34—41)

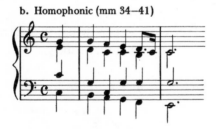

c. Polyphonic (mm 41—50)

Finally, make it clear to students that most music exhibits both vertical (chordal) and linear (melodic) dimensions. For example, a Bach chorale is usually analyzed harmonically and therefore classified as homophonic in texture. Yet, Bach, himself, in the musical tradition of his time conceived of each voice as an independent though closely related line. In this sense, all of his music is polyphonic. The polyphonic approach is validated by the emphasis upon the voice leading of individual parts in the Baroque era. Note the lines of the chorale setting by Bach arranged for band. Listening must be directed to both chords and lines.

Ex. 5—20 *If Thou Be Near* by Bach

The emphasis upon individual lines is also the most important consideration for band members to achieve expressive playing. All important, moving lines must be balanced for valid interpretation.

6

How to Illustrate Structure and Formal Types

The musical materials and elements that have been studied in Chapters 2 through 5 do not exist in isolation. The composer must assemble them according to some organizational plan to achieve coherence and expression in his music. The musical plan is called "form." Studying form is the best way to understand complex, extended compositions and delve into the essence of serious music. In this chapter, the organizational components and formal principles of music are examined and illustrated for presentation in rehearsal. Next, the standard forms of music are studied as they are found in band literature. Finally, a method to analyze music is presented to help students and director examine the formal content of new compositions.

COMPONENTS AND PRINCIPLES OF FORM

Form in music is divisible into two basic components: (1) design and (2) tonal structure. Students must study both to understand fully the construction of a given musical work.

Design

Design refers primarily to the melodic dimension of form. Phrases, themes or sections can be similar (repeated) or different (contrasted). Here we see the ancient Greek aesthetic formula, "unity in variety," at work in music. (1) *Repetition* gives unity to music. The recurrence need not be exact, only similar. As noted earlier, sequence is an example of altered repetition. In a sequence, a motive or phrase is repeated several times on different successive scale steps. Other examples of altered repetition include imitation, variation and development. They will be discussed later in this chapter. (2) *Contrast* refers to the introduction of a new and different motive, phrase, theme, or section. Contrast gives variety and interest to music. *Symmetry* results when the beginning material reappears after the contrasting section.

Have your band listen for similar and different phrases in the following examples. Have them indicate the design by marking the initial phrase or section with an "a," and the contrast with a "b." Limit the analysis to the first complete statement of the theme.

Chester, Billings-Tolmage, (Staff)

Chester Overture, Schuman, (Merion)

Hymn of Brotherhood, Beethoven-Tolmage, (Staff)

Hymn of Freedom, Brahms-Gardner, (Staff)

"Intermezzo" from *English Folk Song Suite,* Vaughan Williams (Boosey)

Irish Tune from County Derry, Grainger, (Fischer)

Londonderry Air, arr. Walters, (Rubank)

"Largo" from *New World Symphony,* Dvorak-Safrenek, (Fischer)

"Largo" from *New World Symphony,* Dvorak-Ortone, (Pro Art)

"St. Anthony Chorale" from *St. Anthony Divertimento,* Haydn-Wilcox, (G. Schirmer)

"Larghetto" from *Military Symphony in F,* Gossec-Goldman, (Mercury)

"Song Without Words" from *Second Suite in F,* Holst, (Boosey)

Ye Banks and Braes O' Bonnie Doon, Grainger, (G. Schirmer)

Tonal structure

"Tonal structure" or "tonal movement" is the harmonic dimension of form. Tonal areas (key centers) and cadences are strong unifying and controlling aspects of formal organization. Cadences, as end points or goals of phrases, are particularly important for the performer. Play over example 6-1 with your group.

Ex. 6–1 "Ode to Joy" theme from *Ninth Symphony* by Beethoven

(arr. Henderson, pub. ProArt) (or "Hymn of Brotherhood", arr. Tolmage, pub. Staff)

Note the incompleteness of measure four, the half cadence. Stop here and ask the students how it makes them feel. Such terms as unstable, unbalanced, tense, inconclusive, incomplete and nonterminal are appropriate answers. The music physically feels as if it should continue. It seems to require the phrase repetition (measures five through eight) with its stable and satisfactory conclusion, the perfect authentic cadence. The first is an "antecedent" phrase that leads to the second "consequent" phrase. Together they form a "parallel period."

New thematic material is presented from measures nine through twelve, again ending on a half cadence. Measure thirteen begins an exact repetition of the second phrase with its conclusive, perfect authentic cadence. Together, the final two phrases constitute a "contrasting period."

The phrase design of the melody is a a' b a'. The tonal structure is I–V, I–V-I; I–V, I–V-I, consisting of one parallel period followed by one contrasting period.

The students should have discovered the following rules of traditional small forms from this example: "Period structure" refers to a grouping of two phrases. The first phrase ends upon an incomplete cadence, usually a half cadence. The harmonic movement is completed by the second phrase which ends upon a stable, conclusive cadence. If the two phrases are melodically similar, the form is a parallel period. If they are melodically dissimilar, they form a contrasting period. When contrasting material is introduced, the original theme or section will be repeated as a general rule forming an A B A design. Of course, not all small forms follow this rigid format. Note the design and tonal structure of the *St. Anthony Chorale* by Haydn.

The five-measure phrases of "a" and the repeated "b" phrases would create an asymmetrical design except for the added, balancing coda. The harmonic structure consists of a parallel period, followed by a contrasting period that has two antecedent phrases and one consequent phrase. The coda simply extends the tonic. The coda is initiated by the elided, perfect authentic cadence. "Elision" results when one section cadences as another begins.

As you perform examples of these small song forms, ask your bandsmen to explain the ways that the contrasting sections (digressions) are different. Here is a list of possibilities.

1. Melodic line (theme)   6. Harmony
2. Rhythm   7. Texture
3. Meter   8. Dynamics
4. Tempo   9. Instrumentation
5. Tonality (key)

Finally, notice that the return of the original theme, the restatement, "rounds off" a composition making it symmetrical. *A B A* at all levels of form, small or large, is symmetrical. Although

St. Anthony Chorale by Haydn

Design	a	a'	:‖ b	b'	a'	Coda :‖
Tonal Structure	I→V (HC)	I→V⁷-I (PAC)	V→V⁷-I (IAC)	IV→V (HC)	I ⟶ V⁷-I---I (PAC) elision	
Measure	1---5	6----10	11----15	16---18	19---22 23---29	

symmetry is not found in all music, it is another fundamental organizing force.

TEACHING FORMAL TYPES

Standard band literature can serve well to illustrate the forms that have evolved in the history of Western musical culture. The first step is to find good examples of the form you want to teach. Then make a schematic drawing of the form that includes design, tonal structure and perhaps the dynamic plan of the work. Have the diagram run off for distribution or make a transparency for use on the overhead projector. Better yet, do both. A transparency can be made easily by running your diagram through a thermofax copier with a blank acetate transparency film. A transparency has certain advantages for teaching since you can point to the section about which you are talking. Putting the schematic drawing on the chalkboard is time-consuming but effective if you cannot obtain an overhead projector. Have reference books handy for student use. See the listing at the end of this chapter.

Binary forms

Binary or two-part form is a sectional design consisting of two complete harmonic movements. Most of the music listed previously in this chapter is binary. In the small binary form each part can consist of nothing more than a phrase as *America.*

America

Design	a	b	‖

Tonal Structure $\quad$ $I \longrightarrow V^7\text{-}I$ $\quad$ $I \longrightarrow V^7\text{-}I$
$\qquad\qquad\qquad\quad$ (PAC) $\qquad\qquad$ (PAC)

Measure $\qquad$ $1\text{-----}6$ $\quad$ $7\text{------}14$

Each part of Grainger's *Irish Tune From County Derry* (the traditional *Londonderry Air)* is in period structure. The design is a a′ b b′; or simply A B. The entire piece is motivically and melodically similar.

Ex. 6–2 *Londonderry Air*

Notice the reference to "a" in the last four measures of Example 6-2. This serves to round off and complete the melody in a musically satisfying way. It also can initiate an academic argument. Have students analyze Example 6-1 and the *St. Anthony Chorale*. Are these works binary or ternary forms? The a b a design suggests three-part form. Yet there are only two tonal movements which indicates two-part form. Compositions such as these are called either "rounded binary" forms or "incipient ternary" forms. Many are constructed from one parallel and one contrasting period.

Traditionally, the first part of binary structure modulates to a closely related key, usually the dominant. Each part is also repeated. The "March" from Purcell's *Air and March* (arr. Gordon, pub. Bourne) provides a good example of baroque binary form.

March by Purcell

Design	A	:‖ B	:‖
Tonal Structure	$I \longrightarrow \overset{V}{\underset{(C)}{}} \text{of } V - \overset{V}{\underset{(F)}{}}$ $B^b \qquad (PAC)$	$I \longrightarrow V^7 - I$	
Measure	1 — — — — — — — —10 11— — — — — — — —20	21 — — — — — 30 31 — — — — — 40	

The classical minuet provides another good source of binary form. Each major section consists of a rounded binary. Use the "Minuet and Trio" from the *Linz Symphony*, Mozart-Beeler (Rubank) or the "Minuet and Trio" from the *Jupiter Symphony*, Mozart-Bake (Pro Art). The *Jupiter Minuet* is outlined here.

The traditional march form is binary in construction (march and trio). Each section is usually binary also. Sousa's *Stars and Stripes Forever* is exemplary.

The march trio traditionally modulates to and remains in the subdominant key. Again the question may arise: "Is the trio a binary or ternary form?"

"Minuet" from <u>Jupiter Symphony</u> by Mozart

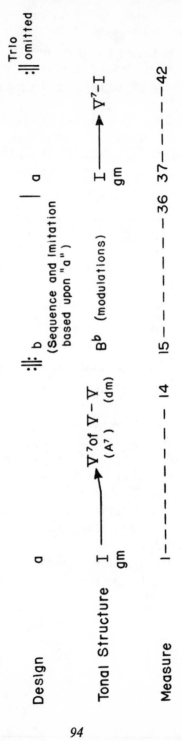

Design   a   :‖: b | a   Trio
                                    (Sequence and Imitation   :‖ omitted
                                    based upon "a")

Tonal Structure   I ──→ V⁷of V – V   Bᵇ (modulations)   I ──→ V⁷– I
                   gm   (A⁷) (dm)   gm

Measure   1 – – – – – – 14   15 – – – – – – 36   37 – – – – 42

Stars and Stripes Forever (March) by Sousa

Design   Intro. ‖: $\overset{A}{a}$ ‖: b   ‖: $\overset{B(trio)}{c}$ ‖: d | c ‖

Tonal Structure

$$I \longrightarrow \underset{(F^7)}{V^7} \text{of } V - \underset{(Bb)}{V} \quad I \longrightarrow V^7 - I \quad I \longrightarrow V^7 I \longrightarrow V^7 \quad I \longrightarrow V^7 - I$$

E^b E^b A^b

Measure   1–4   5– – – – – –20   21– – – –36   37– – –68   69– –72   73– – – –124

Ternary forms

As a general rule, the "true" ternary form is identified by its design and tonal structure: (1) It has three-part design, usually A B A. Each part is independent and thematically important. (2) It has three complete harmonic movements. Deciding whether a work is binary or ternary when the above two conditions are not fully met becomes an academic question. Reference has been made to the rounded binary or incipient ternary. Careful analysis reveals that the binary and ternary forms are complementary—not opposed. Actually, most examples from the literature fall on a continuum between the "textbook" binary and the "textbook" ternary. As someone has said, "Composers hardly ever read the text."

The classical minuet and trio provide the best example of the large ternary form: A (minuet); B (trio); A (minuet-*da capo).* Mention was made earlier that the minuet and trio sections consist of rounded binary forms.

The "Largo" from Dvorak's *New World Symphony* illustrates ternary form on two levels.

The first large "A" section consists of a small extended ternary form.

Rondo

The rondo is a sectional form like the ternary. It may be regarded as an extension of the ternary idea. In the rondo a theme or section (the refrain) is alternated with contrasting themes or sections (episodes). Rondo designs include A B A C A, A B A C A B A, and many others. Episodes usually modulate to closely related keys as well as introduce different thematic material. Haydn's "Rondo" from the *St. Anthony Divertimento* has the basic design A B A C D A Coda. When repeats are taken the design is A B A A B A C C D A D A Coda.

	Binary Form	Rounded Binary Incipient Ternary	Ternary Form
Design	A || B A || A	A || B A	A || B || A
Harmonic Structure	I – V || V – I I – I || I – I	I – V || V – I I – I || V – I I – I || I – I	I – V || V – V || I – I I – I || V – V || I – I

"Largo" from New World Symphony by Dvorak

Design

A	B	A
Intro. a a'b b a a" trans. b b(extended) a a codetta	cdcd trans.	a a'b b a a" coda ‖

Tonal Structure D^b E^b D^b

Measures | — — — — — — — — — — — — — — — 45   46 — — -100   101— — — — 127

"Rondo" from St. Anthony Divertimento by Haydn

Design	A a a' ff period	B |: based upon chorale motive	C :|: phrase group	D :|: based upon chorale motive	A |a a'	Coda :|‖

Tonal Structure: $I \rightarrow V\ I \rightarrow V^2\text{-}I$ (Bb) | $I \rightarrow V$ (gm) | $I \longrightarrow \overset{V\ I(V)}{C^7\ F} \rightarrow I \rightarrow VI \rightarrow V\ I$ (Bb) | $I\text{--}I$ tonic pedal

Measure: 1------8 9----16 17----24 25----32 33----44 45----52 53----60

99

Try some of these rondos with your band and let the students analyze the designs by listening carefully for repetitions and contrasts.

Rondo Giocoso, Erickson (Bourne) [M]
Rondo Marziale, Frankenpohl (Shawnee) [M]
Roundelay for Band, Hardt (Lavell) [E]
Rondo for Band, McLean (Shawnee) [M]
Rondo and Minuet, Mozart-Paulson (Mercury) [M]
Fanfare and Rondo, Purcell-Gardner (Staff) [E]
Prelude and Rondo, Tuthill (Summy-Birchard) [M]
"Finale" from *Royce Hall Suite,* Willan-Teague (Associated) [D]
Fanfare and Rondo, Velke (Shawnee) [M]

Arch form

The arch form is another type of sectional form. Contemporary composers use it extensively because it seems sell suited for the organization of modern musical content. As its name implies it has the shape of an "arch"—A B C B A, A B C D C B A or A B C D E D C B A. The first movement of the Vaughan Williams *English Folk Song Suite* is in arch form.

Theme and variations

"Variation" refers to the repetition of a theme in an altered, ornamented or amplified version. Some of the elements are repeated (held constant) giving unity, while others are ornamented or elaborated resulting in variety. The harmonic progression is often left the same in traditional variations while other elements are altered. The old theme and variation solos of Clark and Pryor illustrate this well. Contemporary free variations as Dello Joio's *Variants on a Medieval Tune* or Schoenberg's *Theme and Variations* are really "developments" of the theme. They are musically more mature, difficult and interesting.

Have your bandsmen listen carefully to the variations they are performing to ascertain which of the elements are held constant and which are varied. The following musical elements and materials can be altered in variations.

"Seventeen Come Sunday" (March) from <u>English Folk Song Suite</u>
by Vaughan Williams

	A	B	C	B	A	
Design	a a	‖ b (b) c b ‖:	d d e d :‖	b (b) c b ‖	a a ‖	Coda ‖
						<u>da capo</u>
Tonal Structure	fm	A♭	fm	A♭	fm	
Measure	1- - -30	31- - - -64	65- - 96	97- -128	1- - -30	

1. Rhythm and tempo	6. Dynamics
2. Melody	7. Instrumentation
3. Bass line or inner parts	8. Key
4. Harmony	9. Mode
5. Texture	10. Form (design or length)

Use any of the many examples available for the band.

> *Theme and Variations,* Beethoven-Reed (Mills) [MD]
> *Variations on a Korean Folk Song,* Chance (Boosey) [MD]
> *Variations on a Shaker Melody,* Copland (Boosey) [M]
> *Variants on a Medieval Tune,* Dello Joio (Marks) [D]
> *Variations on a Theme by Haydn,* Dello Joio (Marks) [D]
> *Enigma Variations,* Elgar-Slocum (Shawnee) [MD]
> *Symphonic Variations,* Franck-Arlen (Kendor) [M]
> "Second Movement" from *Surprise Symphony,* Haydn-Kiser (Hal Leonard) [M]
> *Variations on America,* Ives-Schuman (Merion) [MD]
> *Variations on a Theme,* Pagannini-Gardner (Staff) [ME]
> *Theme and Variations, Op 43a,* Schoenberg (G. Schirmer) [D]
> *Chester Overture,* Schuman (Merion) [MD]
> *Variation Overture,* C. Williams (Ludwig) [E]
> *Diamond Variations,* Jager (Volkwein) [MD]

Sonata-allegro

The sonata-allegro form utilizes all of the organizing principles including development. "Development" refers to a more complex manipulation or working out of a theme than usually connoted by variation. A theme is manipulated through fragmentation, transformation, imitation, modulation, sequence, free counterpoint, inversion, retrograde or altered instrumentation. Unity is achieved through the recurrence of thematic material, with infinite shades of variety possible through manipulation.

The sonata-allegro form consists of three main parts: (1) exposition, (2) development, and (3) recapitulation. In the exposition, two or more contrasting themes are presented. In the development section, the themes are manipulated and tension is built. Usually the climax of the work occurs here. The themes are restated and resolved in the recapitulation in the tonic key. The design and tonal structure of the sonata-allegro form is an elaboration of the rounded binary principle.

Rounded Binary Form

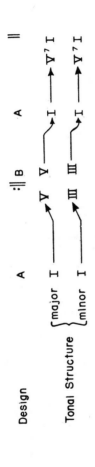

Design A :‖ B A ‖

Tonal Structure
{ major I → V | I → V⁷ I
{ minor I → III | III → V⁷ I

Sonata-allegro Form – Basic Diagram

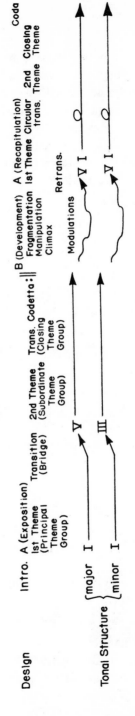

Design

Intro. | A (Exposition) 1st Theme (Principal Theme Group) | Transition (Bridge) | 2nd Theme (Subordinate Theme Group) | Trans. Codetta :‖ (Closing Theme Group) | B (Development) Fragmentation Manipulation Climax | A (Recapitulation) 1st Theme Circular trans. | 2nd Theme | Closing Theme Coda

Retrans.
Modulations

Tonal Structure
{ major I → V I → V I
{ minor I → III V I → V I

Several sonata-allegro compositions for band are analyzed for teaching purposes. *Paradigm* by Sol Berkowitz (pub. Franck) is a jazz oriented work with a complete analysis in all band parts. The "Allegro" from *Minuet and Allegro* by Mozart (arr. Whitney, pub. Alfred) also has an analysis and teaching suggestions included with it. Any work in sonata-allegro form can serve for teaching purposes. The following analysis of Catel's *Overture in C* (pub. Mercury) is exemplary.

Overture in C by Catel

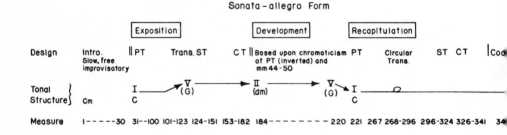

The following list of band compositions are in sonata-allegro form.

"First Movement" *Fifth Symphony*, Beethoven-Godfrey (Chappell) [M]

Egmont, Beethoven-Winterbottom (Boosey) [MD]

Overture in Classic Style, Carter (Bourne) [E]

104

"First and Fourth movements," *Symphony No. 3 For Band,*
Giannini (Columbo) [D]

Russlan and Ludmilla, Glinka-Henning (C. Fischer) [MD]

Classic Overture in C, Gossec-Goldman (Mercury) [MD]

London Symphony, Haydn-Isaac (Belwin) [M]

"First Movement," *Symphony for Band,* Hindemith (Schott)
[D]

Overture in C for Band, Mendelssohn (G. Schirmer) [MD]

Marriage of Figaro, Mozart-Slocum (Mills) [MD]

Titus Overture, Mozart-Moehlman (FitzSimmons) [M]

"First Movement," *Symphony No. 6 for Band,* Persichetti
(Elkan-Vogel) [M]

The Tzar's Bride, Rimsky-Korsakov-Harding (Kjos) [M]

"First Movement," *Unfinished Symphony,* Schubert-Cailliet
(Carl Fischer) [M]

Ostinato forms

The term, "ostinato," literally means "obstinate." It refers to a
persistently repeated musical pattern. Most often an ostinato is
melodic although it may be harmonic or rhythmic in character.
Ostinato forms developed when melodies or variations were
written over, around and "against" the repeated pattern.

One of the earliest ostinato forms utilized a short repeated bass
figure called a ground bass, *basso ostinato* or *cantus firmus,* over
which melodies were written. Use the Couperin, *Cantus Firmus
and Fugue* (arr. Scott, pub. Pro Art) and the Bach "Crucifixus"
from the *Mass in B Minor* (arr. Peterson, pub. Kendor) for
examples.

The passacaglia and chaconne are ostinato variation forms. The
passacaglia uses a repeated melodic line as the fixed element
around which variations are written. This line may shift from voice
to voice. The chaconne consists of a repeated harmonic progression around which the variations are written. Confusion often
arises because composers use these terms interchangeably. The
"Chaconne" from Holst's *First Suite in E Flat* is a good
illustration. Although it is called a chaconne, it is a passacaglia by
definition.

"Chaconne" from First Suite by Holst

	1	2	3	4	5	6	7	8	9	10	11	12	13	14	15	16
Dynamic Curve																
Dynamic Markings	p		cresc. mf		cresc.f	cresc.ff	dim. p						cresc. poco a poco ff			marcato rit.
Theme Statement	1	2	3	4	5	6	7	8	9	10	11 (inverted →)	12	13	14 (extended)	15	16
Theme Played by	bass	bass	bass	bass	bass	bass	brass	brass	horn	a. sax	horn, cl. a. sax	tutti	tutti	tutti	tutti	bass trb.
Var Played by	brass w.w. sus.	w.w.	tutti w.w.	w.w. bass	bass	w.w.	w.w. sus.	w.w.				bass bass	bass	tutti	tutti	tutti
Tonal Structure	E♭									Cm			E♭			
Cadence Type	HC	HC	HC	HC	HC	HC	IAC	HC	PAC	HC			dom. pedal	HC		tonic pedal

Thematic Resolution

Note the use of nonharmonic tones, especially suspensions, in the predominantly polyphonic texture.

As in a typical passacaglia, the Holst ("Chaconne") theme is stated alone by the bass instruments and remains in the bass line through several repetitions. (See figure 6-12.) At measure 9, a legato variation is stated against the theme by brass and continued by the woodwinds. At Ⓐ a *staccato* variation of sixteenths and eighths has fanfare-like qualities. This builds to the sixteenth-note woodwind runs of the variation at letter Ⓑ with the theme in punctuated eighth-note chords. At measure 49, the basses play a running eighth-note variation *pesante* against the theme in the treble. Beginning at Ⓒ, pastoral variations are set against the theme played by horn and then alto sax. At measures 70-72, Holst utilizes the first strong cadence in the tonic key. It releases the tension of the previous half cadences, and prepares the way for the thematic inversion (m 75) and the change of key to the relative minor. The inverted form is found again *pesante* at Ⓓ, with the theme turned "right-side up" beginning in the ninth measure, (but it is transposed up a third). An incessant quarter-note bass line with increasing intervalic skips dominates this section. This is temporarily resolved at Ⓔ where the theme is again stated in the tonic E flat. However, tension mounts through the next two statements by means of a dominant pedal, *crescendo,* ascending harmonies, added sonority, eighth-note movement of inner voices and increasing range. All of this leads to the climactic statement at letter Ⓕ with the melody in the bass instruments. But Holst is not through yet. He achieves complete thematic resolution of the movement by stating the theme "one more time" over a tonic pedal. The theme is also transposed up a fifth to lead inexorably to the final tonic chord.

The "Finale" of the Brahms *Fourth Symphony* (arr. Foote, pub. Kendor) is an excellent example of the chaconne. The composition consists of thirty variations above a repeated eight-measure harmonic pattern followed by a coda. Brahms' accomplishment was degraded by critics who did not "catch on" to the form at the premiere performance.

Use any of the following examples that are appropriate for your band.

Passacaglia and Fugue in C Minor, Bach-Falcone (Southern) [MD]

Passacaglia in G Minor, Bright (Shawnee) [MD]

Passacaglia in E flat, M. Frank (Bourne) [M]
Passacaglia and Fugue, Johnson (Carl Fischer) [M]
Passacaile, Lalande-Beeler (Elkan-Vogel) [E]
Caucasian Passacaglia, Nelhybel (G. Schirmer) [M]
Chaconne, Purcell-Gardner (Staff) [E]
Passacaglia, Alfred Reed (Frank) [M]
"Mass" from *La Fiesta Mexicana,* H. Owen Reed (Summy-
  Birchard) [D]
Passacaglia, Scott-Leist (Galaxy) [MD]

Fugue

The fugue is a monothematic form (or more correctly, technique) in which a theme (fugue subject) is extended and developed by imitation. The fugue begins with a statement of the subject in one voice part alone. The subject is "answered" by another voice part at the interval of a fourth or fifth while the original voice plays a countersubject against it. In an exposition of a four voice fugue, there are two sets of such statements and answers as the theme is restated in a series of successive entrances. A free contrapuntal development follows called an episode. Expositions and episodes follow one another until the fugue ends. As the fugue moves toward its climax, the composer often uses "stretto" to build intensity. Stretto refers to the overlapping of entrances in close succession.

The exposition of the Bach *Fugue in D Minor* (arr. Moehlman, pub. FitzSimmons) extends from m 1 to m 22. The subject (theme) is stated in the tonic D minor by oboes and clarinets, and answered by alto saxes and cornets in the dominant key of A (m 6). The oboes and clarinets continue to play a countersubject. Note the overlapping cadence—the second entrance occurs before the cadence of the first statement. The subject enters again in the tonic (m 11) in tenor sax, horns and trombones, and finally in the bass instruments (m 16). Notice how each line is "colored" by the sounds of the instruments and thus maintains its individual quality. Although this is a transcription of an organ work, the principle of coloring the equal lines of the polyphonic texture was a Baroque technique in direct contrast to the mixing, blending and pointing up of individual instrumental colors that started in the Classical era and was exploited fully in the Romantic period.

Fugue – Basic Diagram

| Exposition | | Episode | (Exposition)(Episode) etc. |

Subject --- Countersubject --- Free Counterpoint -- -- -- --

       Subject -- -- -- --Countersubject ---Free Counterpoint-- --

               Subject-- -- -- -- Countersubject -- --

                           Subject -- -- --

fragmentation
stretto
development

I   V   I   V   Modulation

A development of fragments occurs in the episode (m 22-27), beginning in A minor and modulating to C. An incomplete exposition begins (m 28). The second and third cornets state the subject while the first cornets play the countersubject. Following this, the bass instruments play the subject in a *tutti* passage (m 35-39), beginning in the key of F and modulating to C. At mm 40-47, motives are tossed about in a sequential ascending passage to reach the key of A. At this point, the theme is stated climactically in the alto voice in D minor and answered in the bass which reaches an "A" pedal, above which a long cadential pattern intensifies to the tonic.

Fugue in D Minor by Bach

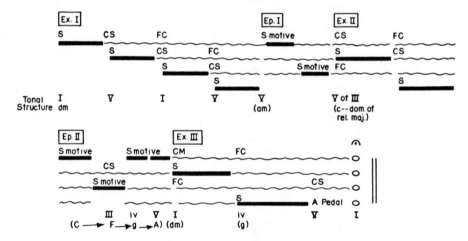

Use any of these additional fugues for band.

Little Fugue in G Minor, Bach-Boyd (Cole) [MD]

Prelude and Fugue in B flat Minor, Bach-Moehlman (Fitz-Simmons) [M]

Prelude and Fugue in F Minor, Bach-Moehlman (FitzSimmons) [M]

Prelude and Fugue in G Minor, Bach-Moehlman (Fitz-Simmons) [M]

Prelude and Fugue in F Minor, Bright (Shawnee) [MD]

Cantus Firmus and Fugue, Couperin-Scott (Pro Art) [E]

Prelude and Fugue, Nelhybel (Frank) [MD]

Fughetta, Stainer-Righter (Schmitt, Hall and McCreary) [ME]

Passacaglia and Fugue in C Minor, Bach-Falcone (Southern) [MD]

Concerto grosso

The *concerto grosso* is a polyphonic form developed in the Baroque era. The "concerto principle" contrasts a small group of instruments—the *concertino*—with the remaining instruments of the orchestra—the *ripieno.* Often they play together—*tutti.* The effect is like a "combo" backed up by a "big band." In a typical *concerto grosso* movement, the *tutti* presents the main theme in the tonic key. After the initial statement, the movement consists of alternations of the *concertino* and *ripieno* parts. The return of the theme in the *ripieno* is called a *ritornello,* which literally means "returning theme." Opening and closing *ritornello* sections are usually complete and self-contained units. The *ritornello* theme is often incomplete in other *ripieno* statements. Modulations and development of fragments from the *ritornello* occur in the *concertino* passages. The theme or motives from it are treated by imitation or sequence. Contrast and variety are achieved principally by the alternating of the sonority of the small and large groups.

Use the Handel *Concerto Grosso* for two flutes, clarinet and band (arr. Malin, pub. Remick). The basic form of the first movement is described here. A complete analysis is found in Chapter 8.

Tutti (mm 1-18): Statement of the main theme, which sounds similar to the "Hallelujah Chorus" in the key of C major. It is treated sequentially through the dominant G and back again to C.

Concertino (mm 19-22): flute figurations based upon theme.

Ripieno (mm 23-24): short *ritornello* modulating to G.

Concertino (mm 25-30): again figurations based upon the theme.

Ripieno (mm 31-32): shortened *ritornello.*

Concertino (mm 33-45): long passage typical of idiomatic writing for the solo instruments, featuring displays of technique.

Ripieno (mm 45-50): sequential melody line cadencing in G.

(mm 57-72): Continued alternation of *concertino* and *ripieno* moving through E Minor.

(m 73): Final *ritornello* in C, which is similar to the first statement but often changing sonority between *tutti, ripieno* and *concertino.*

Other forms

The preceding survey of formal types is obviously not complete. It is intended to provide your bandsmen with a basic background through a selective study of the principal forms.

Forms that have not been covered include the free forms as the symphonic poem, toccata and prelude, and the multiple forms as the suite and the symphony. These can be studied in their historical contexts. See Chapters 8 and 9.

HOW TO ANALYZE MUSIC

Many band works published today provide a formal analysis with the program notes. The value of the analysis varies with its completeness and accuracy. As we have seen, both dimensions of form must be included in a complete analysis—design and harmonic structure. Often the director must do this himself. Both he and his students can follow the steps suggested here for analysis.

Analytical procedure

1. Locate phrases by indicating cadence points and cadence types.

Look particularly for the important divisive cadences that separate the major sections of the work.

2. Mark the design. What is similar (repeated) and what is different (contrasted). In a large composition note the use of development and variation also.

3. Mark the tonal structure. Check cadence types—are they terminal or progressive in function? What are the important key areas? What is the harmonic movement—modulations and return to tonic?

4. Determine if the composition belongs to a standard formal type. Does it coincide with any of the patterns that have been studied?

5. Note the dynamic plan, phrase climaxes and sectional climaxes within the composition for expressive implications. Expressive performance depends upon moving the on-going "line" through to cadence points as dictated by the structure or "shape" of the composition. See Chapter 11.

SELECTED BIBLIOGRAPHY

Berry, Wallace, *Form in Music.* Englewood Cliffs, N.J.: Prentice-Hall, Inc., 1966.

Christ, William, *et. al., Materials and Structure of Music,* Vol. I and II. Englewood Cliffs, N.J.: Prentice-Hall, Inc., 1967.

Green, Douglass M., *Form in Tonal Music.* New York: Holt, Rinehart and Winston, Inc., 1965.

Hodeir, Andre, *The Forms of Music,* Trans. Noel Burch, New York: Walker and Company, 1966.

Reti, Rudolf, *The Thematic Process in Music.* London: Faber and Faber, 1961.

Salzer, Felix, *Structural Hearing.* New York: Charles Boni, 1952.

Spink, Ian, *An Historical Approach to Musical Form.* London: G. Bell and Sons, Ltd., 1967.

Stein, Leon, *Structure and Style.* Evanston, Ill.: Summy-Birchard Company, 1962.

7

How to Enhance
Musicianship by Teaching
General Styles of Music

The finest performing organizations have "style." In the words of the music critic, they "capture" the spirit of the composition in a "convincing" performance. But what does style mean exactly and how does your band acquire it?

The all-inclusive use of the term "style" makes it difficult to define. Style means "fashionable" in popular usage. To be in style is to be in vogue or to be in accord with the current standards of taste—the latest styles in clothing, automobiles or architecture. So-called "popular" music provides another good example of style in this sense. The connotation is usually reversed in "serious" music, however. Style is synonymous with artistic excellence. It is the quality that gives distinctive character and excellence to performance. Style distinguishes the fine performance from the mediocre.

This chapter presents several approaches for teaching style in

114

the full band rehearsal. First, articulation is related to style. Then, the basic styles—*staccato, marcato* and *legato*—are examined. Several techniques are suggested for teaching styles and style markings. Finally, march style and the rubato are discussed.

ARTICULATION AND STYLE

Technically, style in performance is achieved by articulation. Style markings and the musical context determine the degree of connection (or separation) of notes and the appropriate way to start and stop the notes. Everything that follows can be related to this general principle. Figure 7-1 is an articulation-style chart that illustrates this principle graphically.

As a first step, then, the director must demand that his students carefully follow the articulation in their parts. They must tongue and slur exactly as marked in the music. A careless reading results in distortion of the composer's intent as well as a sloppy performance. In Example 7-1 the composer has indicated, as precisely as possible, the articulation and, thus, the style that he wants.

Ex. 7—1 *Second Suite* by Gustav Holst
© Copyright 1922 by Boosey & Company, Ltd. Renewed 1949
Used by permission of Boosey & Hawkes, Inc.

Obviously, the director may wish to alter certain articulations to suit his organization or his conception. For example, a technically difficult, tongued run can be cleaned-up with a "slur two—tongue two" articulation.

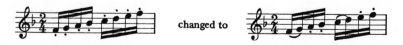

ARTICULATION OF A TONE

Method of Attack

Manner of Release

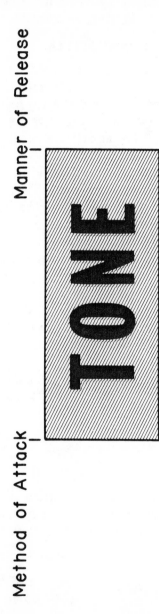

Accented?

Amount of Accent?

Unaccented?

Emphasized?

De-emphasized?

Connected to following note?

Separated from following note?

Degree of separation?

Slight?

Much?

The director may also want to alter articulation markings that are inconsistent with the historical style of the composition. Students should mark the exact changes in their parts. If possible, parts should be edited before rehearsal to save time.

Except for such changes, students must articulate their band music exactly as it is marked for precision and style.

BASIC STYLES OF MUSIC

The Vaughan Williams *English Folk Song Suite* is a fine standard band work that serves well to introduce students to styles of music. Generally, all music can be categorized in one of four basic styles: (1) *leggiero* (light *staccato*), (2) heavy *staccato,* (3) *legato* and (4) *marcato.* [1] The first movement of the *Folk Song Suite* presents each of these styles in clear-cut sections requiring *subito* changes. Have your band rehearse this work to acquaint them with the basic styles. Teaching is made easier with the fine Eastman Wind Ensemble recording, *British Band Classics, Vol. I* (Mercury, MG 50088).

After the four-measure introduction, the first theme is stated *pianissimo,* light *staccato (leggiero).*

Ex. 7–2 *English Folk Song Suite* by Vaughan Williams
Copyright 1924 by Boosey & Company, Ltd. Renewed 1951
Used by permission of Boosey & Hawkes, Inc.

The *leggiero staccato* is a light, separated style indicated by the *staccato* mark (dot).

The theme is repeated *tutti, fortissimo* beginning in measure eighteen in the heavy, *staccato* style.

---

[1] See Max Rudolf, *The Grammar of Conducting.* (New York: G. Schirmer, 1950) for an explanation of these styles in conducting.

Ex. 7–3 (credit as 7–2)

The heavy or full *staccato* style is also indicated by a *staccato* mark in a loud dynamic context.

The style abruptly changes at the coda sign (m 31) to *legato*.

Ex. 7–4 (credit as 7–2)

The *legato* is a smooth, sustained, connected style.

With the pick-up notes to measure sixty-five (at the repeat sign), the style shifts suddenly to *marcato* in the bass-line melody.

Ex. 7–5 (credit as 7–2)

Marcato is a heavy, emphasized style. It is usually accented and separated. *Marcato* literally means "marked." The degree of separation depends upon the musical context. In this example, heaviness is more important than detachment. That is, this passage is to be played in a heavy, full manner with only a slight separation of tones. The march style, by contrast, is the best example of the well-separated *marcato*.

Have your band read the articulation carefully as marked throughout this movement. Note the effective use of the *tenuto* to sustain certain notes for agogic emphasis. Caution the players never to "clip off" the final notes of phrases, even if they are marked *staccato*. Use a breath-release to have final tones "ring-off" musically.

SPECIFIC METHODS FOR TEACHING BASIC STYLES

The following suggestions will help you teach the styles of music to your band.

1. Choose music carefully. Examples like the *English Folk Song Suite* are best for teaching style because the articulation and dynamics are carefully and extensively marked. Attention to markings provides a solid start.

2. Provide a good model to develop conception. The director can sing the style to demonstrate it for the band. This is the most used method to achieve uniformity of style. However, a good recording is the best method of developing conception. The total picture is presented in a clear-cut, impressive way. Reference has been made earlier to effective timing in the use of recordings for teaching. You may wish to use the record initially to provide a model if the group is inexperienced, or wait a few rehearsals to present it as a "clincher."

3. Help students get a physical feel for style. Several years ago I observed Harry Robert Wilson achieve "style" with a young group in a very short time. He used a physical approach. He called *marcato* "punched" music and had the students punching the air to get the feel of it. He described *legato* as "smooth" music and had the students making connected, wave-like motions with their hands. *Staccato* was called "chopped" music. He had the students make choppy motions with their hands (palms facing, fingers together in *karate* fashion). These techniques resulted in a startling improvement of style in performance.

4. Teach your students to follow the stick. Elizabeth Green gives an excellent account of baton technique to achieve style in the performing group. She calls the conducting-training procedure "psychological conducting." [2] A simpler variation of this technique can be used successfully to train your band to follow the stylistic indications of your baton. First, write down a series of quarter-notes in one or more meters; indicate the style by appropriate stylistic and dynamic markings. This is for your own use. The students have no music; they just watch you closely.

---

[2] Elizabeth Green, *The Modern Conductor,* Second Edition. (Englewood Cliffs, New Jersey: Prentice-Hall, Inc., 1969), pp. 231-4.

Ex. 7—5 Quarter-note drills

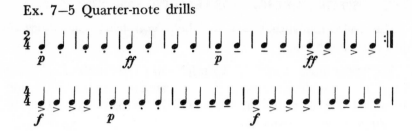

In rehearsal, instruct your students to play quarter-notes the way your baton tells them to play. Use the tonic note, tonic chord, or whatever note you think is appropriate for this drill. We have based quarter-note "compositions" upon the pentatonic scale, the whole-tone scale, and even aleatoric episodes in which students play any pitches they want. The drill can be expanded to include tempo changes, shadings, cut-offs and holds, with or without release.

This training results in greater student awareness of the conductor as style-giver and interpreter. Students learn the visual indications of stylistic symbols. The next section explores these style markings in greater depth.

STUDY THE SYMBOLS OF STYLE

As students advance in the study of style, a more concise definition of style markings is necessary. The many symbols can be understood if their meanings are clarified and applied to the music being rehearsed. A student study sheet is included for basic definitions. A further analysis is provided for the director in the areas that may be ambiguous.

Figure 7-2

STUDENT STUDY SHEET

Articulation and Interpretation

♩ ♩ ♩ ♩ Unmarked notes are articulated in relation to the total musical context. As a general rule, the notes are more connected in slow tempos.

Staccato means to separate the tones. The relative length of the notes is regulated to a large extent again by tempo. *Staccato* may be heavy or light depending upon the dynamic level.

Marcato style is heavy and separated. The degree of separation depends upon context.

Lines over notes have two connotations: legato or tenuto. (1) The *legato* style is smooth, sustained and connected. (2) The *tenuto* style consists of a succession of full, block tones that are intense and definitely separated.

Legato tongue: Use a "du" articulation with no separation of tones.

Slurred *tenuto:* Use a heavy, *legato* tongue with emphasis, intensity and diaphramatic push, but no separation.

Semi-*legato* style: tones are slightly separated, usually without intensity.

The basic definitions of the student study sheet should be clarified in rehearsal. Much confusion results from the use of similar markings in varying contexts. For example

means something different according to the medium employed.

1. Strings—*staccato,* in one direction of the bow
2. Piano—semi-*staccato* (slightly detached)
3. Wind instruments—*legato* tongue

Another illustration that often needs clarification in transcriptions is

1. Strings—*louré* bowing (semi-detached slur, with a tenuto-like quality)
2. Piano—full value and phrasing
3. Wind instruments—heavy *legato* tongue with a breath attack or diaphramatic push on each note

Another confusing example is ♩♩♩♩ . Many arrangers use this marking to indicate *legato*. Technically, the lines in a series indicate *tenuto* style. A *tenuto* style requires full lengths of notes with no accent but a slight separation.

Staccato is often played too short with a labored "tut-tut" articulation. This is often caused by the director shouting "short!!" during *staccato* passages. The better students then overdo what they are told, trying to overcompensate for those players who are not separating. "Spacing" not just "shortness" is the key. Every note must have tone.

HOW TO TEACH MARCH STYLE

The march style is *the* basic band style. It is surprising to find many bands that cannot play a march convincingly because they do not articulate. March style is "spirited." It is achieved by proper spacing and emphasis of notes. It is a disconnected style, except for the *legato* line typified by the trio or lyric counter-melody. Tones in a march are "energetic" (depicting motion).

Here are some general rules:

1. Follow written articulation.
2. Separate.
3. Replace the dot of dotted rhythms with a rest for correct spacing and emphasis.
4. Leave space before accents (♩ ♩ ♩ equals ♩ ♩ ♩

    and ♩ ♩ equals ♩ ♩ ♩).

5. Longer tones receive the most emphasis. Lighten the shorter ones.
6. Play all accents carefully but never lose tone by overblowing them. Overblowing of any type destroys tone quality and style.

TEACHING *RUBATO* STYLE

The subtle use of *rubato* as an expressive device is used in most slow music. However, extensive "give and take" utilized throughout the composition results in the *rubato* style.

The literal translation of *rubato* is "robbed." Musically, it means to dwell upon and prolong the prominant melodic tones and chords. This requires an equivalent acceleration of less important tones, which are thus "robbed" of a portion of their time value. There are two types of *rubato:* the "push-on" *rubato* and the "hanging" *rubato.*[3] (1) In the "push-on" *rubato,* a slight hurrying of the tempo creates agitation through forced movement and intensification. This is necessarily followed by a slowing to the original tempo and release of intensity. (2) In the "hanging" *rubato,* more time is given to an important note or group of notes at the beginning of a phrase. An *accelerando* follows in order to overtake the original tempo. Expressively the intensity is heightened by the initial *tenuto* or *ritenuto.*

Most music from the romantic era requires *rubato.* Grainger's *Ye Banks and Braes O' Bonnie Doon* also provides a good teaching piece for the *rubato* style. The indications for "give and take" are marked into the score by Grainger, himself. See Chapter 11 for this and other examples.

---

[3] Tobias Matthay, *Musical Interpretation.* (Boston: Boston Music Company, 1913). Read all of Section III for an extensive and excellent discussion of *rubato.*

8

How to Teach Historical Styles: Performance Practice

The preceding chapter explained how to perform "with style." However, a valid interpretation must also reflect the historical period in which the music was written. This chapter and the two that follow expand the concept of style to include historical context. Two related aspects of historical style are presented to develop the musicianship of individual students: (1) performance practice and (2) musical characteristics of the era.

"Performance practice" is examined in this chapter. A summary of performance practices is given to teach students how to perform "in the styles" of the Baroque, Classical, Romantic and Contemporary periods. Several projects and programs are suggested. Comparison is used as the teaching device.

DEFINING AND EXPLAINING PERFORMANCE PRACTICE

Performance practice refers to the way that musicians performed music at the time it was written, or more accurately, it refers to the "traditional" or appropriate ways the music is to be performed today. The study of performance practice is appropriate for, and immediately applicable to, the full-band rehearsal. It provides a practical approach to begin the study of historical style periods.

Ask your students questions such as these to initiate thinking and out-of-class research. What is a valid interpretation? How should the Haydn *March for the Prince of Wales* be performed? How would it differ from the performance of Wagner's *Die Meistersinger March*? How were these compositions first performed? Although these questions may be difficult to answer concisely, directors make frequent judgments about the style of performance both in and out of rehearsal. Think about the recordings of the Haydn *Trumpet Concerto* by Al Hirt and Helmut Wobitsch. Which recording is more stylistically valid? Is either recording "authentic"? It brings to mind a band I once adjudicated that played the opening horn and trumpet theme from the "Finale" of Dvorak's *New World Symphony* in a severely detached march style, instead of the heavy, but less detached *marcato* emphasis that is more characteristic of the Romantic era.

At this point, the perceptive director might well ask if there can ever be a valid performance of an orchestral transcription by a band. As one band director commented, "How can a classical symphony be given an authentic reading by a 120-piece symphonic band?" The truth is that "authentic" performances are impossible anyway. There have been many musicological attempts to "recreate" performances by duplicating original conditions. However, such performances are usually quite sterile musically. They create dusty museum pieces instead of vital, living music. Think again about the Haydn *Trumpet Concerto* played this time on an antique, natural (valveless) E flat trumpet. The performance would sound more quaint or odd to our ears than authentic, although it would have sounded "right" to Haydn's contemporaries.

The solution is not to be found at the other extreme, either. The performer should not "romanticize" or "jazz-up" the work to meet modern taste—even though, as stated before, we cannot help but view all music in relation to our time. Perhaps there is a sensible middle-ground that the director can take. The ideal is to capture the spirit of the music in its historical context and characterize it with appropriate performance. This can be taught to the band through exemplary literature. Therefore, the director must accept transcriptions with reservations and modifications to complete the band's historical repertory.

For the individual band student, style often implies restrictions, because what may be acceptable or appropriate regarding articulation, dynamics, tone quality, rhythm, tempo, agogics and phrasing for one historical period may be entirely inappropriate for another. The performer must study performance practice to determine what is proper in a given style. He must project himself back, so to speak, to capture the *zeitgeist,* the spirit of the times, and reflect this in his performance.

The following outline summarizes the traditions of performance practices. Like all generalizations, they may be half-truths when applied to any specific composition. Still, they provide the student and the director with guidance toward a valid interpretation. The areas of articulation, dynamics, tone and rhythm are especially important for the individual student.

How to play the Baroque style

1. Articulation

Generally, articulation is heavy with full note values. However, in faster tempos the longer notes should be separated slightly for correct style. Shorter notes are not separated.

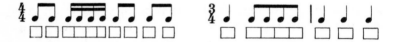

This articulation is not a true *staccato.* The dynamic level and full quality of all the notes must remain even. Fast notes should not be lightened and separated as in the Classical *staccato.* This does not mean that they should be overblown. Instead, the full tones of the organ or detaché bowing (each note played on one direction of bow) should be simulated.

Slow movements are played very *legato* with a "weighted" feeling.

2. Dynamics

Very few dynamic markings are found in original Baroque manuscripts although it can be assumed dynamics were consistently used in performance. Traditionally, "terrace dynamics" are appropriate for this style. Terrace dynamics are large blocks of stable dynamic levels that alternate between loud and soft. When sections are repeated, it is also traditional to use the opposite dynamic level; for example, *forte* the first time and *piano* on the repeat.

Long *crescendos* and *diminuendos* are not traditionally used, but arrangers and editors often write them into transcriptions. They must not be overdone or romanticized. Subtler shadings are appropriate for slow movements.

3. Tone

Tone quality is full and heavy for the block-note style. It is not the sonorous, "lush" color associated with the Romantic era, however. Keep the sound of the pipe organ in mind.

4. Rhythm and Tempo

Baroque music should be performed with a strong emphasis upon the beat. Tempos are steady and driving. The on-going rhythmic effect is often described as "motoric." Dotted notes are traditionally interpreted as double-dotted (♩. ♪ equals ♩.. ♪).

5. Melody

As a general rule, emphasize the melodic line and the bass line. The bass is especially active and important in this style. It should be strong and heavy. However, contrapuntal lines must be balanced. They are of equal importance.

6. Orchestration

Delete all percussion parts except the tympani. Other parts may require thinning for balance in some transcriptions of suites and *concerto grossos*. Transcriptions of organ works are usually suitable as they are.

How to play the Classical style

1. Articulation

Classical articulation is very light, refined and concise. Students must develop a light, crisp, controlled *staccato*. It should never sound like a labored "tut-tut." Have students use the tip of the tongue and think of the bouncing, *spiccato* bowing for a guide. Never clip off final notes even if they are marked *staccato*. Have them "ring off" for the sake of tone. Often students play a final *staccato* note as a harsh attack followed by a forced release with no tone in between.

2. Dynamics

Have students read dynamics carefully, but underplay all dynamic levels. Do not overblow accents. Accents should be approached as "emphasis," never as a literal explosive or labored force of tone. *Sf, sfz* and the various accent marks simply indicate a stress one degree louder than the dynamic context.

The strong-beat emphasis of a dissonant note that resolves on a weak beat is common in the Classical style. When this occurs at the end of a phrase it is called a feminine cadence. Always stress the first note and sustain the second at a weaker dynamic level, creating a heavy to light effect (♩ ♩ never ♩ ♪ 𝄽).

Crescendos and *diminuendos* must be carefully controlled for gradual intensification of tone, but they should not be overdone or romanticized.

3. Tone

Tone quality should be light, clear, pure and "transparent," but not "thin" in the sense of lacking tone. Restraint is the watchword.

4. Rhythm and Tempo

The measure rather than the beat is the important metric unit. Tradition demands an emphasis upon the first beat of the measure. The tempo "bounces" along in a rather straightforward manner. Strive for rhythmic exactness, precision and control.

5. Melody

The melody should stand out in the predominantly homophonic texture. Play melodic lines one dynamic degree louder for projection and balance. Conversely, play accompanying parts one dynamic level softer than written. Practicing scales and arpeggios helps develop the needed technique for this essentially diatonic style.

6. Orchestration

The Classical orchestra was small. Parts may have to be thinned in band transcriptions. Most percussion parts should be deleted. Consult the original score for the correct percussion parts and for ideas about thinning or rescoring sections. The "bugling-type" trumpet parts and diatonic horn parts reflect the limitations of the natural instruments. These parts must be played in a light, subdued style.

How to play the Romantic style

1. Articulation

Articulation is heavy and intense. In general, notes are held full, block value. Follow articulation markings carefully.

2. Dynamics

A wide range of dynamics are utilized in this style. Work for control of at least the six basic dynamic levels; *crescendos* and *diminuendos* can be practiced "by the numbers." Long crescendos must be carefully controlled and "fed" in Romantic compositions to gradually intensify the line. Unexpected and explosive *sforzandos* must be executed precisely for their color effect. Small shadings and nuances are an integral part of the style. Have students read all dynamic indications carefully and follow them exactly for balance and expression.

3. Tone

Romantic tone quality is rich, full and sonorous. It is heavier and more intense than in the Classical period. Vibrato–judiciously applied—is appropriate for intensification, color and warmth.

4. Rhythm and Tempo

Rhythmic exactness and precision may be sacrificed for the expressive effect of the *rubato* and the long phrase. Students must follow carefully the "give and take" of the conductor pushing the phrase to climax and cadence.

5. Melody

The Romanticists were lyricists, so melodies must sing. Good breath control is needed to play the long melodic lines. Practicing chromatic scales helps develop needed techinque for this age of chromaticism.

6. Orchestration

The Romantic composer used a large orchestra and wanted a big mass of sound, especially from the brasses. Instrumental colors were exploited, both individually and in combination. Thus, bring out the "sounds"!

How to play the Contemporary style

The Contemporary era consists of a confusing diversity of styles, some quite traditional and some *avant-garde*. Much of the so-called "school music" that bands play is traditional. Think of all the typical Romantic "rehashes" in the repertory. The musical elements and forms are used in much the same way as they were in the Eighteenth and Nineteenth Centuries. This music is interpreted traditionally.

Avant-garde, experimental and other "authentic" Contemporary music is difficult to interpret because it has no tradition. Often good recordings can serve as guides. As a general rule, the performer should follow the articulation, dynamic markings and rhythmic notation exactly as written to achieve a straightforward rendering of the composer's intentions. Most Contemporary compositions should not be over-Romanticized. The Contemporary reaction against Nineteenth Century Romanticism tends to manifest itself in Classical ideals. However, the individual work must dictate the exact interpretation.

The Contemporary emphasis upon percussion is quite evident in much modern band literature. The percussion section in today's bands must be well trained and well equipped, and the parts well rehearsed.

Further discussion and examples of diverse Contemporary styles are found in Chapter 9.

PROJECTS COMPARING PERFORMANCE PRACTICES

Although the historical styles have been listed chronologically in the preceding discussion, it is not necessary to study them in that order. Reverse chronology is another possible approach. Often it is better to begin where the students are, perhaps with music that is well liked and known to the band. In this way, initial information is immediate and appropriate. In the suggested projects that follow, the order of musical presentation is not important. However, comparison of the musical compositions *is* important. Comparison is the most effective method for teaching style to the band. Specific information from the preceding outline is contrasted. The projects have worked well for teaching performance practice and for concert programming.

The dramatic overture through the ages

One band director explained how he set up a concert featuring a succession of overtures from different historical periods. The overtures included Handel's *Messiah,* Mozart's *The Marriage of Figaro,* Wagner's *Die Meistersinger* and Gershwin's *Porgy and Bess.*

He said the program had great audience appeal and gave him an opportunity to explain to his students how style affects the total sound of the band. He had to tell his band (1) how and why the tone quality of the *Figaro* is so different from *Porgy and Bess;* (2) similarly, how and why the brasses must play differently in the *Figaro* as opposed to *Die Meistersinger;* (3) how the dotted rhythms are played differently in the Handel, Mozart and the Gershwin; and (4) why the harmony is so simple and basic in the Mozart, and so complex and chromatic in the Wagner.

Follow the outline to set up your own program from the sample compositions listed here.

1. Baroque
   Purcell-Walker, *Dido and Aeneas,* Kjos
   Handel-Cailliet, *Overture to the Messiah,* Boosey and Hawkes
2. Classical
   Haydn-DeRubertis, *Orlando Palandrino Overture,* Remick
   Mozart-Barnes, *Impresario Overture,* Remick
   Mozart-Slocum, *Overture to the Marriage of Figaro,* Mills
3. Romantic
   Wagner-Winterbottom, *Overture to Die Meistersinger,* Boosey
      and Hawkes
   Wagner-Osterling, *Die Meistersinger Excerpts,* Ludwig
   Wagner-Drum, *Prelude to Act III of Lohengrin,* C. Fischer
4. Contemporary
   Gershwin-Bennett, *Porgy and Bess,* Gershwin Pub.
   Bernstein-Beeler, *Overture to Candide,* G. Schirmer
   Bernstein-Gilmore, *Prologue from West Side Story,* G. Schirmer

The march through the ages

A similar approach can be taken by tracing the history of the march. Marches have tremendous audience appeal. Here are some sample compositions.

1. Baroque
   Purcell-Gordon, *Air and March,* Bourne
2. Classical
   Haydn-Riley, *March for the Prince of Wales,* G. Schirmer
3. Romantic
   Berlioz-Leidzen, *March to the Scaffold,* C. Fischer
   Wagner-Winterbottom, *Homage March,* Boosey and Hawkes

4. Contemporary
   Sousa, King and Fillmore Marches
   Osterling, *The Nutmeggers,* Bourne
   Holst-Jacob, *Moorside March,* Boosey and Hawkes
   Shostakovich-Suchoff, *Fortinbras March,* MCA Music

The concerto grosso, then and now

The *concerto grosso* developed in the Baroque era, but many Contemporary composers have used this form in interesting ways. Using forms of the past is called "Neo-classicism." A program that utilizes a Baroque *concerto grosso,* a Contemporary *concerto grosso* and a Dixieland *concerto grosso* can be used effectively for a lesson in dotted rhythms.

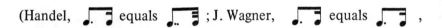

(Handel, ♩. ♪ equals ♪. ♪ ; J. Wagner, ♩. ♪ equals ♩. ♪ ,

Warrington, ♩. ♪ equals ♩ ♪ .

1. Baroque
   Handel-Malin, *Concerto Grosso,* Remick
   Vivaldi-Cacavas, *Concerto Grosso,* Chappell
2. Contemporary
   Bright, *Concerto Grosso,* Shawnee
   Joseph Wagner, *Concerto Grosso,* Remick
   Morrissey, *Concerto Grosso,* Chappell
   Warrington, *Original Dixieland Concerto,* Marks
   Warrington, *Tailgate Concerto,* Chappell

The prelude and fugue, then and now

As the *concerto grosso,* the prelude and fugue that developed in the Baroque era can be compared to Contemporary examples of the form.

1. Baroque
   Bach-Moehlman, *Prelude and Fugue* (in G, D, or F minor), FitzSimmons
   Bach-Boyd, *Little Fugue in G Minor,* Cole
   Handel-Osterling, *Prelude and Fughetta,* Ludwig
2. Contemporary
   Bright, *Prelude and Fugue,* Shawnee
   Nelyhbel, *Prelude and Fugue,* Frank

9

How to Teach the Historical Styles: Musical Characteristics

Correct performance practice is the logical first step for teaching bandsmen a concept of historical style. Teaching style improves the band's performance. It develops precision through stylistic concensus. It is essential for valid interpretation. It even saves rehearsal time in the long run. Once styles are learned, new music can be related quickly to the correct performance practice.

This chapter is devoted to another complementary approach to style that provides the background knowledge for the "performance feel" discussed in Chapter 8. It also develops musicianship through a deeper understanding of the music played. It concentrates upon the distinctive musical characteristics of musical compositions from each of the historical periods. Composers of every age had their characteristic ways of manipulating the materials and elements of music, and of constructing their forms.

Information about the timbre, elements and forms of the Baroque, Classical, Romantic and Contemporary periods is presented for the busy band director to incorporate into his rehearsals. The materials can be easily developed into student study sheets that summarize musical style characteristics. Several representative projects are suggested. Lists of exemplary band literature are also provided.

THE BAROQUE ERA (c. 1600-1750)

General characteristics

The term "Baroque" was first used in a derogatory sense to designate the period of the "figured bass." [1] It was derived from the Portugese "barocco," an irregular or imperfect pearl. It is interesting to note that by Classical standards this period was indeed imperfect or irregular. At worst, the music was bombastic, over-elaborate, grandiose, theatrical, and several other adjectives usually reserved for Hollywood spectaculars. However, this is because it was not judged by its own values.

The monumental proportions of the High (late) Baroque music resulted in extremely complex, large scale and yet magnificent compositions. The dominance of the sacred over the secular also influenced the type of music composed. Much of Baroque music was composed for the church, whereas most Classical music was composed for the court.

Melody

Baroque instrumental melodies tend to be long, florid and ornamented. The melodic line is spun out in sequences, as in Example 9-1, and/or imitation, as in the fugue. Phrase structure is often irregular with no marked feeling of cadence.

Ex. 9—1 *Concerto Grosso* by Handel

Baroque composition is usually monothematic. That is, only one theme or "affect" (mood) dominates the composition or section. The fugue is again a good example.

---

[1] "Figured bass," "thorough bass" or "basso continuo" all refer to the 17th and 18th Century practice of improvising chords on the harpsichord to fill in the harmony above the written bass part. Numbers below the bass notes indicated the harmony to use. In band transcriptions, the arranger "realizes" the figured bass by filling in appropriate harmony.

Harmony

Baroque music is tonal, written in either a major or minor key. The harmony is functional for it clearly defines key centers. Chords change frequently, resulting in fast harmonic rhythm and strong harmonic drive. The bass line is quite active, heavy, strong and important. Harmonic cadences are infrequent. Overlapping cadences and elision are used extensively for this effect. Elision refers to the simultaneous ending of one phrase and beginning of the next phrase; thus, no real "break" occurs.

Ex. 9–2 Concerto Grosso by Handel

Rhythm and articulation

Baroque music is metric, with a strong emphasis upon the beat. Tempos are steady and driving with a traditional *ritardando* at the final cadence. Slow movements are quite *legato*, yet "weighted" in feel. In the faster movements, articulation is heavy with full note values, yet there is slight separation of longer notes for correct style.

Ex. 9–3 Concerto Grosso by Handel

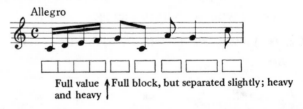

Dotted notes are often performed as double-dotted in the Baroque tradition (♩. ♪ equals ♩.. ♪ and ♪. ♪ equals

).

Ex. 9—4 *Messiah Overture* by Handel

Where triplets predominate in the music and in compound meters, composers often notated ♩. ♪ to mean ♩ ♪.

Dynamics

Baroque composers seldom wrote dynamic indications into their music, although it can be assumed that dynamics were used. In general, "terrace dynamics" are appropriate for this style. Terrace dynamics are large blocks of stable dynamic levels that alternate between loud and soft. They result naturally from the alternation of large and small instrumental groups as in the *concerto grosso,* and from the different manuals of the organ.

Long *crescendos* and *diminuendos* are extremely rare, but arrangers and editors often write them into band transcriptions. Subtle shadings are appropriate in slow movements.

Texture

The High Baroque is the period of tonal polyphony. The fugue and other contrapuntal forms were developed. Some homophonic music is found, as, for example, the chorale. However, all music of this era was conceived polyphonically. Thus, each part should be performed as a melodic line.

The sonority is heavy and thick.

Instrumentation

The strings, harpsichord and organ were the important instruments of this era. The winds were still quite crude in construction, although flutes (and recorders), oboes and bassoons were used quite extensively. There was also a virtuoso tradition on the natural trumpet, i.e., a trumpet with no valves. Trombones were considered church instruments.

In general, Baroque composers used what instruments they had on hand, and "colored" the equal contrapuntal lines of the polyphonic texture so each would be clearly heard. This can be likened to the use of contrasting organ manuals to give each musical line a distinctive quality.

Transcriptions, especially of organ works, are quite effective for the band.

Ornamentation

Ornamentation is one of the improvisatory characteristics of the Baroque style. Ornamentation refers to added notes in the form of trills, mordents, appogiaturas and turns.

The trill is traditionally approached from above and resolved with a turn.

Ex. 9—5 *Messiah Overture* by Handel

Most ornaments in band transcriptions are written out by arrangers. Several are given below for illustration.

Ex. 9—6

Shake or   (single   Turn
Inverted Mordent   trill)

Appogiaturas (N.B. these are not "grace notes" and they are played on the beat)

Form

Baroque form is usually monothematic in construction. One theme is used throughout the complete composition or a major section of the composition. Thus it is well integrated and unified. However, it lacks contrast by Classical standards. Baroque form also depends upon functional harmonic arrangement—(1) a strong statement of the tonic key at the outset, (2) departure from that key, and (3) a return to the tonic key. Strong cadences are usually reserved to define important formal divisions.

Important formal types include the *concerto grosso,* fugue, *chaconne, passacaglia,* suite (dance forms), opera, oratorio, and improvisatory forms, as the toccata, fantasia and prelude. (See Chapter 6.)

Important Composers

J.S. Bach (1685-1750), Handel (1685-1759), Vivaldi (1680-1743), Corelli (1653-1713), Frescobaldi (1585-1644), Purcell (1658-1695).

Compositions

Bach-Moehlman, *Preludes and Fugues* (Bb, F, G and D minor), FitzSimmons. [M]

Bach-Falcone, *Passacaglia and Fugue in C Minor,* Southern. [MD]

Bach-Boyd, *Little Fugue in G Minor,* Cole [MD]

Bach-Leidzen, *Toccata and Fugue in D Minor,* Fischer [D]

Bach-Peterson, *Crucifixus,* Kendor (*Passacaglia*) [M]

Couperin-Scott, *Cantus Firmus and Fugue,* Pro Art [E]

Frescobaldi-Slocum, *Toccata,* Mills [M]

Handel-Malin, *Concerto Grosso,* Remick [MD]

Handel-Johnson, *Messiah Overture,* Rubank (French overture) [M]

Handel-Cailliet, *Messiah Overture,* Boosey (French overture) [M]

Handel-Osterling, *Prelude and Fughetta,* Ludwig [ME]

Handel-Ades, *Hallelujah Chorus,* Shawnee [M]

Handel-Johnson, *Hallelujah Chorus,* Rubank [M]

Handel-Sartorius, *Royal Fireworks Music,* Mercury (Suite, binary forms) [M]

Handel-Harty, *The Royal Fireworks,* Chappell [D]

Handel-Kay, *Water Music,* Presser (Suite, binary forms) [M]

Purcell-Gordon, *Air and March,* Bourne [E]

Vivaldi-Cacavas, *Concerto Grosso in D Minor,* Chappell [M]

Vivaldi-Lang, *Concerto for Two Trumpets,* Columbo [MD]

Projects

Student study sheets can contain whatever pertinent information you wish. Figures 9-1 and 9-2 emphasize form and performance.

Figure 9-1

STUDENT STUDY SHEET

Air and *March* by Purcell

FORM

Both the *Air* and *March* are good examples of Baroque binary (two-part) form.

Design   A   :||:   B   :||

Tonal Structure I–V   I–V⁷-I

The repeats are written out in score and parts with changes of instrumentation used to effect dynamic contrast and varied color in the repetitions. Usually the section is loud the first time and soft the second time (terrace dynamics).

COMPOSITIONAL TECHNIQUES

1. Note the use of imitation between melody and bass.
2. Note the use of sequence.
    a. *Air* - measures 1,3, and 5 in the melody.
    b. *March* - at rehearsal numbers 9 and 11 in the melody.
3. Note the types of cadences and the use of suspensions and anticipations.

PERFORMANCE

1. Follow the written dynamic level carefully. However, do not make too much out of the *crescendos* and *diminuendos*. These were written in by the arranger. Use terrace dynamics instead. Subtle shadings are appropriate for the *Air*.
2. Do not over-play the notes marked with accents. Just emphasize them. "Sit on them," don't "smack them."

Figure 9-2

STUDENT STUDY SHEET

"Adagio and Allegro" from *Concerto Grosso* by Vivaldi,
Op. 3, No. 11

FORM

Adagio (tutti)	*Allegro*	
[mm 1-6] homophonic	Fugal exposition (tutti) [mm 7-46]	
(block chords	SUBJECT	ANSWER	SUBJECT
are very slightly	[mm 7-15]	[mm 15-23]	[mm 23-31]
separated)	I (Dm)	V	I
	Basses	Cl. & Sax.	Cornets
		Counter-	Scale
		subject in	sequence
		basses	in basses

ANSWER	*Episode*	*Concertino*
[mm 31-39]	[mm 39-46]	[mm 47-63]
V	(cadence on I	Oboe, cl., bssn.
Fl. & Cl.	ending the fugue)	Brass fill in the
		harpsichord, harmony
		(figured bass) V

Tutti	*Concertino*	*Tutti*
[mm 63-95]	[mm 95-111]	[mm 111 to end]
		Cadences: m 115-V
Cadences:		m 139-I; Notice
m 84-I		the long, dominant
m 95-IV		pedal, mm 115-139,
		that helps inten-
		sity build to
		tonic resolution.

PERFORMANCE

1. Staccato marks must never be interpreted as light, classical
   staccato. See Chapter 8, *How to Play Baroque Style*

2. Accent marks must not be over-played. Emphasize and slightly separate in a block-tone style.
3. Terrace dynamics should be used—blocks of louds and softs.

Recorded on Vanguard, BG 572/4A

THE CLASSICAL ERA (c. 1750-1820)

General characteristics

By definition, "classical" refers to the time-honored artistic principles of the ancient Greek masters, who achieved formal clarity through objectivity, simplicity, restraint, and balance. The composers of the late Eighteenth Century, the "Age of Reason," incorporated these ideals in their music. They strove for perfection of form, and their expressive ends were achieved through the manipulation of musical structure. Their compositions are "pure" or "absolute" music.

Two basic trends can be identified in this period. (1) The *Style galant* or "rococo" style is reflective of the aristocratic court. It is light, delicate, gay, refined, spirited, precise, restrained, graceful and/or elegant. At best, it exhibits a controlled, balanced formal simplicity and clarity. At worst, it represents a superficial degeneration of Baroque ornamented style. (2) The *Empfindsamer stil* (sensitive style) or "bourgeois style" is a direct contrast. This style emphasizes dissonance, chromaticism, dynamic color, and the minor mode, along with such dramatic melodic devices as the action-reaction phrase, melodic "sigh" and expectant pauses. Both trends influenced the important composers. The latter led toward musical Romanticism.

Melody

Classical themes are often tuneful and folk-like in character. Melodies are constructed in short symmetrical phrases with frequent cadences, often resulting in period structure.

Ex. 9—7 *Military Symphony for Band* by Gossec

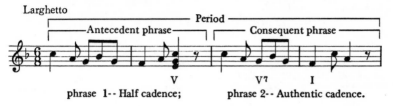

Usually phrases (as well as longer and shorter sections) are constructed in the form of a dialogue. This can be described with such terms as statement-answer, action-reaction, or antecedent-consequent.

Ex. 9—8a *Jupiter Symphony* by Mozart

Ex. 9—8b *March for the Prince of Wales* by Haydn

Unlike Baroque, thematic contrast is utilized in formal design.

Harmony

Classical harmony is tonal—key centered and functional. It is basic and simple. Chords do not change as often as in Baroque music. This results in slow harmonic rhythm. Melody is emphasized in Classical music. Harmony is used simply as a "prop" to support it. The bass line is static. Important harmonic changes occur at the barlines. Repeated chords or repeated chord-tone patterns (arpeggios) keep the rhythmic motion going (Ex. 9-9).

Ex. 9—9 *St. Anthony Divertimento* by Haydn

Cadences occur frequently. The feminine cadence is used extensively (Ex. 9-10).

Ex. 9—10 "Menutto" from *Toy Symphony*
by Leopold Mozart

In the feminine cadence, the dominant seventh chord occurs on the strong beat and resolves on the weak beat over the tonic pedal.

Always interpret the dissonance to consonance as heavy to light or stress to release. 𝅘𝅥 𝅘𝅥 never 𝅘𝅥 𝅘𝅥. As a general rule, never "back away" from dissonance or it will sound like a mistake.

Modulations are to closely related keys and often occur through the cycle of fifths.

Rhythm and articulation

Classical music is metric. The measure rather than the beat is the important metric unit. Classical clarity requires rhythmic exactness, careful control and light, concise articulation. Precision can never be achieved without rhythmic accuracy. Uneven runs are one such problem. Since technical passages in Classical music are usually scale passages, scale study is good to develop technique and facility.

The light, crisp *staccato* style is best exemplified by *spiccato* bowing (the bouncing bow). If tempos in band transcriptions are too fast to achieve an even, controlled, light *staccato,* the "slur two—tongue two" articulation will usually give the effect.

Remember, however, never to clip off the final note of the phrase. Even if it is marked *staccato* or accented, it must be "rounded off." (♩ = ◻ ; never ◻–"tut") Final notes must have body and "ring." They should never sound like a heavy attack followed by a heavy release with no tone in between.

Dynamics

Short-range block dynamics are used to follow the action-reaction phrase structure. Aggressive statements are loud; meek answers are soft. Other dynamics are used increasingly for expressive purposes. These include *crescendo, diminuendo,* nuance (smaller shadings) and the *sforzando.* The *sf* and *sfz* should be interpreted as an accent (>), which receives an emphasis one degree louder than the written dynamic level. This should never be interpreted as a literal explosive or labored force of tone. Tone quality in general is light and clear.

Since dynamic markings are the same in all parts, melodic lines must be played one dynamic degree louder and harmony parts one dynamic degree softer than they are marked. This helps attain Classical clarity through melodic projection. The brass and percussion must be especially controlled.

Texture

Classical compositions are usually homophonic in texture—melody with supporting harmony. However, counter-melodies are used frequently, suggesting polyphonic texture. Polyphony is also used in the development of themes and motives.

The sonority is generally light, thin, clear and transparent.

Instrumentation

The classical orchestra was a small group consisting of a string section with pairs of winds and tympani—two each of flutes, oboes, clarinets, bassoons, french horns, trumpets and tympani.

The individual and collective colors of the woodwinds and horns were contrasted with the strings, while the trumpets and tympani were reserved for the big climaxes. The natural brasses played only a few notes. Their parts are simple, basic and rhythmic in character. Woodwinds were improving in facility. Their parts are more technical. The clarinet was developed and used for the first time in this era.

In band transcriptions, the light, transparent quality must be captured through careful control of tone and dynamics. Restraint is the watchword, especially for brass and percussion. Original band works from this period must also be played in this style.

Ornamentation

The frequent use of ornamentation was carried over from the Baroque. Both new and old practices can be found. By about 1800, the trill was initiated on the written note. Also, grace notes were performed immediately prior to the beat as well as on the beat. The use of the "slash" was one indication. (♪ = prior to beat; ♪ = on the beat.)

Form

Classical composers emphasized structure, the manipulation of musical materials. The small forms generally exhibit regular phrases, period structure, balanced design and clear demarcation of formal sections. With larger works, impressive forms are built up from seemingly insignificant musical elements and motives. To the Classicist, the material was less important then what was done with it. The Romanticist, on the other hand, emphasized the musical material itself. (See "Romantic Era.")

The classical composers retained the Baroque key relationships in most of their forms. However, musical design, especially contrast and development, became more important. Often, as in the sonata-allegro form, two or more contrasting themes were used. This polythematic approach (using two or more "affects" or moods) was directly opposite to the monothematic tradition of the Baroque. Furthermore, the Classicists used transition passages to bridge from one theme, key, mood or style to the other. Development is used extensively. Successive formal sections grow organically in motivic and thematic evolution. The *"First Movement"* of Beethoven's *Fifth Symphony* illustrates this discussion well.

Important formal types include the sonata-allegro, sonatina, rondo, song form, symphony, concerto, overture, theme and variations, suite, opera, minuet and trio.

Important Composers

Mozart (1756-1791), Haydn (1732-1809), Gluck (1714-1787), Beethoven (1770-1827), Catel (1773-1830), Gossec (1734-1829).

Compositions

Catel-Goldman, *Overture in C,* Mercury [MD]
Gossec-Goldman, *Classic Overture in C,* Mercury [MD]
Gossec-Goldman, *Military Symphony in F,* Mercury [M]
Gossec-Townsend, *Suite for Band,* Columbo [M]
Jadin-Townsend, *Overture in F,* Columbo [M]
Jadin-Schaefer, *Symphonie for Band,* Shawnee [M]
Haydn-Isaac, *London Symphony,* "First Mvt.," Belwin [M]
Haydn-Erickson, "Finale" from *Oxford Symphony,* Belwin [M]
Haydn-Gordon, *Largo and Menuetto,* Bourne [ME]
Haydn-Kiser, "Second Mvt.," from *Surprise Symphony*, Barnhouse [M]
Haydn-DeRubertis, *Orlando Palandrino Overture,* Remick [M]
Haydn-Riley, *March for the Prince of Wales,* G. Schirmer [M]
Haydn-Wilcox, *St. Anthony Divertimento,* G. Schirmer [M]
Leopold Mozart-Gordon, *Toy Symphony,* Carl Fischer [E]
Mozart-Baker, "Menuet and Trio" *from Jupiter Symphony,* Pro Art [M]
Mozart-Beeler, "Menuet and Trio," *from Linz Symphony,* Rubank [ME]
Mozart-Gordon, *Alleluia,* Kendor (trumpet solo) [M]
Mozart-Isaac, *Abduction from the Seraglio,* Belwin [ME]
Mozart-Moehlmann, *Titus Overture,* FitzSimmons[M]
Mozart-Slocum, *Marriage of Figaro Overture,* Mills [MD]
Mozart-Tolmage, "Menuetto," from *Symphony No. 39,* Staff [ME]

Figure 9-3

STUDENT STUDY SHEET

March for the Prince of Wales by Haydn

FORM

Large song form (three-part form, A B A).
Each large section consists of a binary form.

Design

A		B(trio)		A
a :‖: b :‖		c :‖ d :‖		D.S. al fine
(two themes) (two themes)				

Tonal Structure   I———▸Ⅴ   I – – – Ⅴ⁷I   I———▸Ⅴ   I--Ⅴ⁷I
                  Eᵇ   (Eᵇ)

(Repeats are written out in score and parts)

COMPOSITIONAL TECHNIQUES

Much thematic and motivic relationship
1. ♩. ♪ motive permeates entire composition
2. Triadic themes on E flat ♩. ♪ ♩ descending; ♩ ♩ ♩ ascending).
3. A descending scale figure is also used throughout. (The scale ascends at the end of the "A" section.)
4. A modified scale theme, used in sequence, dominates the trio. Note the arpeggiated accompaniment.
5. Generally short, symmetrical phrases

PERFORMANCE

Review the performance practice of the Classical style.

Figure 9-4

THE ROMANTIC ERA (c. 1820-1900)

General characteristics

Romanticism in music began its rise at the end of the Eighteenth Century and became predominant in the Nineteenth Century. It paralleled the rise of the individual in society. The worth and dignity of the individual found its highest expression in the American and French Revolutions. No longer did the individual exist for the state, church, or other social institution. Instead, these institutions now existed principally for him. The formalism of the court suited the Classic, but the individualism and imagination of the *man* suited the Romantic.

Romantic music can be described as lyric, complex, dark, heavy, and intense. The style characteristics include subjectivity, lack of restraint, escape from reality, and mixing of art media. Composers preferred emotionalism, programmatic content, and works on a grand scale to Classical finish, proportion and absolutism. They often abandoned the accepted formal patterns and types, and instead emphasized the direct, sensuous impact of musical materials. They worked with sounds for sounds' sake and for coloristic effect.

Melody

The Romantic period is an age of lyricism or as Wagner called it, "unending melody." Mozart, as the Classical master of melody, was the inspriational model. In contrast to the Classical, however, phrases tend to be long and irregular in length. Phrases and themes are often repeated at different intervals creating long sequences which are nonfunctional in the Baroque sense. They have no apparent key function. They exist over and over to be savored for their own sake.

Themes tend to be complex, chromatic and often developed from short motives. Theme transformation is used extensively.

Harmony

Romantic music is basically tonal although definite key feeling is often obscured. The harmony is complex and emphasizes imaginative harmonic color. Harmonic color is achieved by dissonance, chromatic harmony, parallel chords, and other nonfunctional harmonic progressions. Dissonance as a coloristic and expressive device is created by added tones, seventh and ninth chords, altered chords, diminished and augmented chords. Foreign and sudden modulations, especially by third relationship, are used for tension and coloristic effect.

Rhythm and articulation

Romantic music is metric but large rhythmic groupings are emphasized. Many rhythmic effects are used for color as, for example, displaced accents, tempo *rubato* and larger tempo changes. Long tension *accelerandos* are used to heighten expression. Rhythmic precision may be sacrificed for the expressive effect of the *rubato*.

Articulation is heavy and intense.

Dynamics

Romantic composers use dynamics extensively and effectively. They also utilize a wider range of dynamics than Classical composers. Long *crescendos* and *diminuendos* correspond to the rise and fall of emotional tension. Unexpected *sforzandos* are used for emotional and color effects. Small nuances and expressive shadings are carefully utilized in lyric passages. Parts are balanced by appropriate dynamic indications for clarity of expression.

Romantic composers also use a total dynamic plan in their compositions. This large "dynamic curve" consists of ever-increasing patterns of tonal swells or waves to ever-larger areas of climax. The music keeps building and building in intensity.

The band must work for careful control of dynamics within a wide range. Read all dynamics and follow them exactly for balance and expression.

Texture

Romantic music is essentially homophonic. However, nonimitative polyphony often results from the active, moving inner lines.

Instrumentation

Wind instruments were improved mechanically in the Nineteenth Century. The "Boehm system" was used on flutes and clarinets, giving them better facility, range and intonation. Valves were introduced on brasses. For the first time, all brasses could play the complete chromatic compass. Adolf Sax invented the saxophone in Brussels about 1840. He also developed the "saxhorns" which include the baritone horn and tuba.

The result of mechanical improvement and invention was an emphasis upon instruments, their color and virtuosity. Berlioz and Rimsky-Korsakov wrote treatises on instrumentation and orchestration. Wagner, as well as other Romantic composers, did much to exploit the individual and collective color potential of the winds.

Much of Romantic music transcribes well for band because of the emphasis upon winds, especially brass. The brass parts reflect the emancipation that valves brought. Romantic music is performed with heavier and fuller tone than Classical. This is congruent with the increased size of groups, thicker harmony, heavy sonority and extensive use of brass and percussion. Vibrato is appropriate for intensification of tone.

Form

The Romanticists either expanded or rejected the Classical forms. In either case, they emphasized the musical materials with greater impact and length. They exploited the direct sensuous effect of the materials and elements as such—the sounds of melodies (lyricism); the sounds of chords and dissonances (harmonic color); the sounds of instruments playing the melodies and harmonies (orchestration); and the sounds of rhythms and dynamics for their immediate coloristic effects.

Composers utilized long sequential repetition of motives and themes with accompanying dynamic waves of intensification. Often this replaced Classical development. Theme transformation was used extensively. The total result was hugeness and formlessness in the Classical sense.

Important formal types include the music drama, symphonic poem, symphonic variations, virtuoso concerto, symphony, songs.

Important Composers

Wagner (1813-1883), Brahms (1833-1897), Tchaikovsky (1840-1893), Liszt (1811-1886), Berlioz (1803-1869), Schumann (1810-1856), Mendelssohn (1809-1847), Franck (1822-1890), Schubert (1797-1828).

Compositions

The band repertory abounds with examples of Romantic music. Most transcriptions are of this vintage. For this reason the listing here is very selective.

Brahms-Fote, "Finale," from *Symphony No. 4,* Kendor [MD]
Franck-Arlen, *Symphonic Variations,* Kendor [M]
Franck-Harding, *Psyché and Éros,* Kjos (Tone poem) [M]
Liszt-Duthoit, *Les Preludes,* Boosey (Tone poem) [D]
Liszt-Norman, *Les Preludes,* Staff (Tone poem) [M]
Rimsky-Korsakov-Duthoit, *Polonaise,* Boosey [M]
Smetana-Nelhybel, *Three Revolutionary Marches,* Columbo [M]
Wagner-Buehlman, *Traume,* Rubank [E]
Wagner-Cailliet, *Elsa's Procession,* Remick [MD]
Wagner-Cailliet, *Siegfried's Rhine Journey,* Remick [MD]
Wagner-Johnson, *Album Leaf,* Rubank [E]
Wagner-Osterling, *Die Meistersinger Excerpts,* Ludwig [M]
Wagner-Osterling, *Rienzi Excerpts,* Ludwig [M]
Wagner-Whear, *Siegfried's Funeral Music,* Ludwig [ME]
Wagner-Leidzen, *Trauersinfonie,* AMP [M]

Projects

One approach to Romanticism is through the study of the works of Richard Wagner. No composer embodied the spirit of Romanticism in his life and music more than Wagner. His music dramas were an attempt to combine all of the arts in a perfect union. However, his music has attested to the futility of his dream. The *music* has dominated, and in concert form has always been an important part of the band's standard repertory.

The "Prelude" *to Tristan and Isolde* illustrates the heighth of Romantic harmonic tension, chromaticism, and color. There are successions of dissonant chords but never a traditional resolution. The musical line progresses forward, but not to cadence, in the sense of Classical music. The result is a sensuous sonority of harmonic intensity presented by expressive instrumental color. Within this context Wagner's "endless" melody unfolds. Thus, the *Prelude* also illustrates the heighth of Romantic lyricism. Themes are built up of motives (Wagnerian *leitmotifs*) that have literal meaning in the opera plot. The *leitmotifs* found in the *Prelude* are

"Desire" (m 1), "The Glance" (m 17), "Love Potion" (m 25), and "Deliverance by Death" (m 63). This motivic material also helps to unify the otherwise formless flow of harmonic instability and tension. In this way, the motives have structural as well as dramatic functions.

The *Prelude* can be analyzed formally in terms of a dynamic curve. The music gradually builds to a climax (m 83) at which time the opening motives are restated. Lesser climaxes occur along the way, and the denouement is complete after the final climax. (See Chapter 10 for a diagram of the dynamic curve of Franck's *Psyché and Éros.*)

The famous "Tristan chord" (m 2) has been the subject of theoretical and artistic interest since *Tristan's* premiere. It is unanalyzable as a chord in the traditional tonal structure.

"Traume," also adopted from *Tristan and Isolde,* is a much easier arrangement for band. Chromatic harmonies, dissonances, dynamic shading and a theme scored for flutes appear above an A flat pedal that dominates the first section (mm 1-32). The middle section (mm 33-67) is more active, more dissonant and chromatic. The thematic material is built upon the dotted-eighth and sixteenth figure of the first section. The pedal reappears and the quiet of the opening resumes (m 68) to the end.

The traditional harmonic content is expanded by Wagner's use of the appogiatura above the pedal. For example, in measure 11 the following chord is found (excluding the pedal):

This chord resolves in the next measure when the F moves to the E flat root. If the pedal A flat is heard as a chord tone, the effect is even more striking. It illustrates the piling-up of notes in thirds to form larger chords.

Liszt's *Les Preludes* provides an interesting study in theme transformation. Theme transformation refers to the use of the same melodic shape in different meters, rhythms, tempos, voices and/or instruments to change the expression but retain thematic unity. *Les Preludes* is based upon the same motivic idea throughout its seemingly contrasting sections. Even though each section has programmatic meaning in this tone poem, the thematic affinity and theme transformation result in an introduction (theme a), exposition (themes b, c and d), development (themes e and f), recapitulation (themes g and d) and coda (theme h). Thus, it becomes roughly analogous to a sonata-allegro form (Ex. 9-11).

Ex. 9—11

The Holst *First Suite* is another example of theme transformation. Each movement is "founded" upon the same melodic shape. Holst suggests in the score that the suite be "played right through without a break" for this reason.

THE CONTEMPORARY PERIOD (c. 1900-TO THE PRESENT)

General characteristics

The Contemporary era began as all previous artistic epochs as a revolution. The sentiment and overemotionalism of the German-dominated Romantic style did not appeal to growing nationalistic feelings and to new Twentieth Century ideals. Unlike most other breaks, however, a great diversity of styles emerged. Contemporary trends in serious music include Neoromanticism, Impressionism, Nationalism, Expressionism, serial composition, Neoclassicism, jazz, computer music, aleatory music, electronic music, and many forms of experimentation. Perhaps we are just too close to see any one direction that modern music is taking. Some believe that electronic music is *the* music of the future. (*Spectrum* by Bielawa is an available composition for prepared tape and band.)

Diffusion seems to be the norm. Certainly, this age of technology has resulted in an all-encompassing approach to Contemporary serious music. Today as no time before, musicians and scholars have access to almost unlimited information about the music of the past. One composer friend has dubbed these modern times as the "Era of the Musicologist," in the sense that much more musical knowledge is available to the practicing composer because of expanded musicological research. Composers are emulating the past. They are systematically and thoroughly studying the forms and techniques of former eras, assimilating them and incorporating them in their music. The Neoclassical style, best exemplified by Igor Stravinsky, has certainly utilized the musicological approach to study the musical forms and compositional techniques not just of the Classical period, but Baroque, Renaissance, Medieval and even earlier styles. This dominance of research and analysis has the cart before the horse, so to speak. In earlier times, composers wrote the music, then theorists came along to point out the rules and principles based upon compositional practice. Now, however, composers assimilate the theories and compose music based upon them. The result is an unique and personal synthesis based upon the old and new. No wonder there is a confusing hodge-podge characterizing the Contemporary musical scene.

Melody

Contemporary melodies and themes contrast markedly with the usual conception of "melody" as exemplified by Romantic lyricism. Themes are terse, fragmented, motivic, angular, disjunct, modal or serial in construction. They oppose Romantic sentimentalism.

Harmony

Contemporary harmony is dissonant and experimental. Dissonant harmony represents an extension of romantic practice although now it seems to be prized for its own sake, as, for example, unresolved dissonance or dissonance saturation. Harmonic experiments include building chords in intervals of fourths or fifths (instead of thirds), using tone clusters, polytonality (using two or more keys simultaneously), neomodality (using ancient scales), serial organization (the twelve-tone technique), and computer music.

Rhythm

New rhythmic usage includes shifted accents, polymeter and changing meter. The latter refers to multimetric music in which meters change frequently. The beat or a division of the beat remains constant throughout.

Dynamics

Dynamics are used extensively and carefully in varied ways. The performer must follow them exactly.

Texture

The linear (polyphonic) texture prevails in modern serious music. Generally, sonority is thin and "transparent" in contrast to Romanticism.

Instrumentation

Instruments are essentially the same as in the Romantic period. Many novel combinations have been tried. There is a contemporary emphasis upon the percussion.

A standard band instrumentation has been established, and the wind ensemble is becoming an important force in serious music. Today, composers are writing significant works for the band and other combinations of winds.

New methods of sound generation are being used in addition to the traditional instruments. Electronic sources are especially important. The Moog synthesizer is one example.

Form

The forms of modern music are diverse. Serial technique provides one important means of organization. Composers often use formal types from the past in new and unique ways (Neoclassicism).

Composers, trends and compositions

The following survey of late Nineteenth and Twentieth Century trends—the important "isms" and representative composers and compositions—will help clarify the contemporary musical scene.

Neoromanticism. Continuing Romantic ideals.

Hanson-Garland, *Merry Mount Suite,* Carl Fischer [MD]
Hanson-Maddy, *Nordic Symphony,* "Second Mvt.," C.C. Birchard [MD]
Hanson, *Chorale and Alleluia,* Carl Fischer [MD]
Mahler-Gardner, "March," *from Symphony No. 2,* Staff [ME]
Saint-Saens-deRubertis, "Finale," *from Symphony No. 1,* Witmark [MD]
Strauss-Davis, *Allerseelen,* Ludwig [M]
Strauss-Harding, "Finale," *to Death and Transfiguration,* Kjos [M]
Other Composers: Mahler, Bruckner, Barber, Sibelius

Nationalism. Emphasizing national or regional resources and folk music.

Bartok-Suchoff, *Four Pieces for Band,* Sam Fox [E]
Holst, *First Suite in E Flat,* Boosey [M]

Holst, *Second Suite in F,* Boosey [MD]
Milhaud, *Suite Française,* Leeds [D]
Grainger, *Lincolnshire Posey,* G. Schirmer [D]
Grainger, *Hill Song No. 2,* G. Schirmer [D]
Grainger, *Ye Banks and Braes O' Bonnie Doon,* G. Schirmer [E]
Vaughan Williams, *English Folk Song Suite,* Boosey [M]
Shostakovich-Righter, *Finale, Symphony No. 5,* Boosey [D]
Sibelius-Cailliet, *Finlandia,* Carl Fischer [MD]
Other Composers: French Six, Russian Five, Kodaly, Dvorak

Barbarism and Primitivism. Emphasizing the pagan, savage and primitive.

Stravinsky-Wilson, "Berceuse" from *Firebird Suite,* Presser [M]
Stravinsky-Gardner, *Petruska Themes,* Staff [M]
Stravinsky-Gardner, *Danse Infernal,* Staff [M]

Impressionism. Veiled, vague musical impressions of images, e.g., clouds, or the sea.

Debussy-Walker, *Arabesque,* Berkeley [M]
Debussy-Beeler, *Clair de Lune,* Southern [M]
Debussy-Schaefer, "Fetes" from *Three Nocturnes,* Belwin [D]
Debussy-Johnson, *Reverie,* Rubank [M]
Debussy-Wilson, *In Moonlight,* C. Fischer [M]
Griffes-Erickson, *The White Peacock,* G. Schirmer [MD]
DeFalla-Morrisey, *Ritual Fire Dance,* Marks [M]
Ravel-Johnson, *Pavane,* Rubank [ME]
Respighi, *The Pines of the Appian Way,* Colombo [MD]
Ravel-Erickson, *Bolero,* Elkan-Vogel [M]

Expressionism and Serial Music. Musical expressions of intense, inner emotions; the subconscious, Freudianism. More recently, the use of the twelve-tone technique of musical organization.

Schoenberg, *Theme and Variations, Op. 43a,* G. Schirmer [D]
Erickson, *Three Miniatures,* Chappell [M]
Latham, *Dodecaphonic Set,* Barnhouse [M]
Smith, *Somersault,* Frank [M]
Starer, *Dirge for Band,* Leeds [M]

Schuller, *Meditation,* Associated [D]
Other Composers: Berg, Webern, Krenek

   Neoclassicism. Using the forms of the past and Classical ideals in modern compositions.

Bright, *Concerto Grosso,* Shawnee (fl., Ob., C.) [MD]
Bright, *Prelude and Fugue in F Minor,* Shawnee [MD]
Carter, *Overture in Classical Style,* Bourne [E]
Giannini, *Symphony No. 3,* Colombo [D]
Hindemith, *Symphony for Band,* Schott [D]
Ives-Schuman, *Variations on America,* Merion [MD]
Joseph Wagner, *Concerto Grosso,* Remick (2 fl., Cl.) [MD]
Morrissey, *Concerto Grosso,* Chappell (2 trpt., trb.) [M]
Nelhybel, *Prelude and Fugue,* Frank [M]
Perschetti, *Symphony for Band,* Elkan Vogel [D]
Prokofiev-Lang, "Gavotte," from *Classical Symphony*, Mills [ME]
Schuman, *Chester Overture,* Merion [MD]
Stravinsky-Erickson, *A Stravinsky Suite,* Chappell [ME]
Vaughan Williams, *Toccata Marziale,* Boosey [D]
White, *Miniature Set for Band,* Shawnee (Polytonal) [MD]

   Jazz. The use of the jazz idiom in serious composition.

Berkowitz, *Paradigm,* Frank [MD]
Bernstein-Beeler, *Overture to Candide,* E.C. Schirmer [MD]
Bernstein-Gilmore, "Prologue," from *West Side Story,* G. Schirmer [MD]
Copland-Lang, "Celebration Dance," from *Billy the Kid,* Boosey [MD]
Copland-Lang, "Waltz," from *Billy the Kid,* Boosey [M]
Gershwin-Krance, *American in Paris,* MPH [M]
Gershwin-Bennett, *Porgy and Bess,* Gershwin [MD]
Gershwin-Grofe, *Rhapsody in Blue,* Harms [M]
Gershwin-Krance, *Second Prelude,* MPH [M]
Ward-Steinman, *Jazz Tangents,* Sam Fox [D]
Other Composers: Milhaud, Schuler

Aleatoric. Music resulting from chance or improvisatory procedures.

Gillis, *Instant Music,* Frank [M]
Smith, *Take a Chance,* Frank [M]

Experimentalism. The use of novel methods and materials for musical expression, e.g., electronic music or computer music.

Bielawa, *Spectrum,* Shawnee (Prepared tape and band) [MD]
Erb, *Stargazing,* Presser (Prepared tape and band) [M]
Other Composers: Cage, Cowell, Boulez, Babbitt, Varese, Ussachevsky, Luenning

Projects

Many contemporary band works contain teaching suggestions or extensive program notes and analyses. The Frank publications have excellent lesson plans in their "Adventures in Form" series. The themes, rows and forms can be indicated for the works being studied.

STUDENT STUDY SHEET

Four Pieces For Band by Bela Bartok

1. NATIONALISM IN MUSIC

Nationalistic composers used indigenous folk music of their countries in an effort to overcome the dominance of the Romantic, Germanic tradition. Bela Bartok and his associate, Zoltan Kodaly, identified, codified, and utilized the folk music of their native Hungary in their compositions.

2. MODAL, HUNGARIAN FOLK MUSIC

The *Four Pieces for Band* are settings of authentic Hungarian folk songs by Bartok. The melodies are modal but the harmonizations are Bartok and contemporary.

3. UNUSUAL SETTINGS–NEOCLASSICISM

a. Bartok utilizes seventh chords, open fifths and unexpected progressions in the harmonizations.

b. Imitation is used in first and second movements.

c. Ostinato (or "ground bass") is used in third and fourth movements.

d. Inversion (or "mirror") is used in second movement.

Figure 9-5

STUDENT STUDY SHEET

Miniature Set for Band by Donald White

Polytonality is a Twentieth Century harmonic device. It is often achieved when chords are piled up in thirds, creating eleventh or thirteenth chords. Donald White's approach is somewhat different. The cornet and trombone parts in the first movement are dissonant because of the bitonal construction. They are literally written in two different keys. Practicing each section individually will facilitate tuning, analysis, and understanding. The brass parts in the final movement should also be practiced this way.

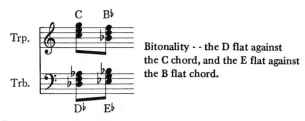

Bitonality - - the D flat against the C chord, and the E flat against the B flat chord.

© Copyright 1964. Templeton Publishing Co., Inc.
Sole Selling Agent: Shawnee Press, Inc., Delaware Gap; Pa. 18327

The *Miniature Set* is also a good study in polymeter. The use of cross rhythms and displaced accents in Romantic music finally gave way in the Twentieth Century to the mixing of meters and uneven meters— 2/4 to 3/8 to 3/4 to 3/8 where the eighth-note is constant. See the first movement, measures 110-14. To keep the eighth-note steady, count: 1&2&, 1&&, 1&2&3&, 1&&.

The form of the first movement is an A B A with some development in the retransition (final A section). The thin sonority, rhythmic complexity, and strident quality (dissonance through bitonality) are all characteristics of contemporary music.

10

How to Teach the Historical Styles: Comparing Musical Characteristics

The preceding chapter has presented an historical overview of the important periods of instrumental music. In this chapter, specific strategies are presented for teaching stylistic characteristics through analysis and comparison.

To teach historical styles, analyze and compare representative examples from each major style period and note the differences in their respective elements and forms. Comparison is recommended as the most effective teaching device. Performing and comparing exemplary scores reveal stylistic characteristics as well as implications for performance. Help students analyze the elements (rhythm, melody, harmony and texture) and the forms of the period. For example, students can compare one melody with another—the short, symmetrical phrases of the Classical with the long, irregular, sequential lines of the Baroque. In this way, analytical knowledge can be very helpful for understanding style.

Follow these steps to get started.

1. Select one or more original band compositions or transcriptions that exemplify each of the four major styles being studied—Baroque, Classical, Romantic, and Contemporary.
2. Begin rehearsing as you would normally. Try to read through each composition initially to get a general conception. If it is too difficult to sight read, use a recording. Then, begin working out problems of technique and intonation as well as basic aspects of style.
3. Study the score further and annotate the places that best illustrate the historical style. Analyze the form. Prepare student study sheets like those developed later in this chapter. Use a style chart for comparisons (See Figure 10-1).
4. In rehearsal, compare the use of one or more of the elements or the form of one composition with another composition from a different style period. Play a section from one composition that illustrates the structural element being considered. Then, play a section from another composition for comparison. Call attention to differences, or ask students to listen for themselves and discriminate. See Chapter 1, How To Present Music.

You can effectively incorporate style study when "tearing down" a section for special rehearsal. Problems of rhythmic accuracy, precision, articulation, phrasing, dynamics, tempo, key, tone quality, balance, and blend are often most easily identified, explained and corrected in a stylistic context. For example, the *staccato* articulation will not merely mean a short or choppy "tut-tut," nor will an accent mark mean a literal explosion if the bandsmen have a conception through listening, analysis, and performance of the light, precise restrained style of the classical period.

PROJECTS COMPARING ELEMENTS AND FORMS

Historical periods should be studied through literature being played, with a minimum of the non-musical and "life stories" considerations. Instead, the director and students should concentrate upon relevant information about the music—structural characteristics, elements, form, instrumentation, dynamics—and the relationship of these to style and performance.

Figure 10-1
MUSICAL STYLE CHART

Period Name	Musical Forms	Materials	Qualities	Composers
Baroque 1600-1750	concerto grosso fugue chaconne, passacaglia suite opera oratorio	melodic sequence long, irregular phrases imitation monothematic figured bass tonal polyphony terrace dynamics	florid heavy monumental complex	Bach Handel Vivaldi Corelli Frescobaldi Purcell
Classical 1750-1820	sonata-allegro rondo song form symphony concerto theme & variations	short symmetrical phrase action-reaction phrase simple harmony light articulation homophonic	light thin restrained gay delicate	Mozart Haydn Gluck Gossec Beethoven
Romantic 1820-1900	symphonic poem music drama symphonic variations concerto symphony overture	lyricism long sequences chromatic harmony harmonic color heavy articulation instrumental color wide dynamic range	heavy thick dark intense complex programmatic	Wagner Brahms Tchaikovsky Liszt Berlioz Mendelssohn Franck Schubert
Contemporary 1900-	neoclassic forms serial organization computer music free-form jazz multi-division of ensemble	melodic fragmentation dissonance saturation polytonality atonality linear polymeter changing meters multi-forces, textures and densities of sounds	thin strident rhythmic abstract	Stravinsky Bartok Schoenberg Hindemith Shostakovich Milhaud Wm. Schumann Persichetti

Classical compared to Romantic

The presentation on the following pages contrasts the Classical and Romantic periods through exemplary compositions. "Classical" and "Romantic" are basic ideals and moving forces in the arts of all ages. The historical periods that bear the names are prime examples of these forces and studying the materials and forms illustrate them best. Biographies of composers and other peripheral information can be assigned to students if additional out-of-class work is desired.

Classical music can best be categorized as "head music," music that is rational, objective, pure, or absolute. It appeals predominantly to the intellect. By contrast, Romantic music has been called "heart music," music that is subjective, and appeals in a more direct, sensuous and feelingful way. The Classicist strove for perfection of form since his expressive ends were achieved through the manipulation of musical structure. The Romanticist, on the other hand, sacrificed the accepted formal patterns and types, and instead emphasized the direct sensuous impact of musical materials. He worked with sounds for sounds' sake.

The Jadin *Symphonie for Band* and Franck *Psyché and Éros* provide good examples of these styles. As a general impression, the first is light, straightforward and somewhat "square," lacking the intense, heavy qualities of the second. However, a structural similarity makes an interesting point of departure for analysis. Both are constructed motivically from the same basic materials: the triad and a three note scale pattern. Differences result from the way the composers used these building blocks, e.g., harmonic structure, modulation, chromaticism, motivic development and theme transformation. Figure 10-2 provides an extensive comparison.

Figure 10-2

MELODY

Symphonie for Band

1. Short phrases of regular length; often just two measures.
2. Periodicy—frequent cadencing.
3. Action-reaction (dialogue) phrase structure.
   a. PT (mm 1-9). Loud-soft effect achieved through orchestration.
   b. ST (mm 24-31). Question-answer (antecedent-consequent) achieved through period structure. First phrase cadences on dominant (mm 24-27) and second phrase on tonic (mm 28-31) similar melodic line, thus parallel period heightened by dynamic contrast.
4. Themes are triadic or diatonic in construction.

Psyché and Eros

1. Long phrases, often of irregular length.
2. No cadencing, melodies run from one into another. Romantic concept of unending melody.
3. On-going evolutionary structure of themes. From a static beginning the theme "grows" or evolves from the minor third interval of the horn and the E flat triad first sounded by the low reeds. Themes are all built up from sequential statements of the motives or their retrogrades.
4. Themes are triadic or diatonic in construction, but chromaticism, and use of seventh chords move melodies through many successive modulations.

HARMONY

Symphonie for Band

1. Simple and straightforward.
   a. Triadic, with normal root movement. Often tonic (F) to dominant (C), as at beginning.

Psyché and Eros

1. Complex and imaginative.
   a. Color effect and dissonance achieved by many altered chords and chromaticism Note the use of the

half-diminished seventh at the beginning. Rather than a dissonant-tensional sound, the soft level of the A^7 is one of static expectancy.

b. Foreign and sudden modulations, often by third relations. (See form chart, second theme.)

c. Chromaticism (mm 25-32, mm 45-48 and mm 139-142, etc.)

b. Expected modulations for the formal design of sonata-allegro. In the development the modulation centers upon the relative minor keys of the dominant and tonic, i.e., A and D minor. In mm 118-128, Jadin employs the "cycle of fifths," a common modulatory device of the Classical era. The suspensions add even more intensity. Note the use of the half-diminished seventh (mm 131-135) in a secondary-dominant function, quite different than the beginning of *Psyché*.

2. (mm 96-104 in development) The A pedal used as a tensional device.

3. (mm 10-11, and all similar places) Play accented passing tone "heavy," resolution, "light." Most student players tend to do the reverse.

2. (mm 55-66) The C pedal helps intensify the first climax.

3. The upper neighboring tone (m 14 and m 16) must be given the nuance carefully as marked for expressive tensional effect.

TEMPO

1. Tempo should be maintained in a regular and steady meter until *rit.* at end. Watch for rushing.

1. *Tempo rubato* throughout with many variations marked, e.g., *animato* (m 45), *Largemente* (m 55) *accelerando* (m 68 and 76). Knowledge of form is the best guide to tempo "agogics." Pull the phrase line to where it's going, then slacken.

2. Play dotted-eighth and sixteenth rhythms precisely with separation.
3. Sustain final notes full value.

TEXTURE

1. Homophonic, some polyphonic feeling in the development.

ORCHESTRATION (SCORING)

1. Essentially a contrast of full band sonority with colors of woodwind solos or mixed woodwind groups. Brass color is utilized more in the development.

DYNAMICS

1. Basically a short-range back and forth dynamic scheme.
   a. Although *fortissimos* are marked, the dynamic norm must be low. The climaxes must be reserved for the

2. Rhythms must not be distorted within the rubato framework. (Rushing or not giving full value to rhythmic figures is a problem.) Follow the conductor carefully so that runs and arpeggios are played together.

TEXTURE

1. Generally homophonic. However, motivic development and active inner lines often result in a polyphonic texture. (See mm 118-125. Note melody and bassoon lines mm 80-93 and mm 158-171.)

ORCHESTRATION (SCORING)

1. Soloistic and sectional colors are exploited for expressive purposes. Note particularly the effective scoring of the beginning and the ending.

DYNAMICS

1. The formal design of *Psyché and Éros* can be described in terms of a dynamic curve. The music moves in gradual swells or waves and builds from lesser to greater

end of the development (m 136) and the final chord (m 200).

b. Smaller nuances are appropriate (mm 10, 11, 31, 32, etc.) for the accented passing tones.

climaxes. The first climax (m 55f) is preceded by increasing waves (m 25, 28, and 41f). The major climax (m 142f) is also preceded by several lesser climaxes (m 102 and m 110). The crucial drive to final climax begins pianissimo (m 114).

ARTICULATION

1. Well separated; crisp, clear *staccato*. Close attention to all marks of articulation.

1. Legato, sostenuto, heavy and intense.

FORM

1. "Abridged" sonata-allegro form. Usually symphonies of the Classical era are multi-movement forms, the first movement of which is in sonata-allegro form. The Jadin work thus seems more typical of a classical operatic overture. However, there is no story to be conveyed; the meaning resides in the musical structure. The "abridged" designation refers to the omission of the principal theme group from the recapitulation.

1. Free form. This is one of four movements originally scored for orchestra by Franck from his oratorio *Psyché and Eros*. It serves, however, as a complete "symphonic poem" in its own right, and as a symphonic poem tells a story. The program is based upon Greek mythology and follows the music: "Love's theme, at first hesitant, becomes bold. After agitated passages and movements of calm, Psyché and Eros ascend to higher regions together and ecstasy comes at last." Thematically, at least, love conquers all.

Jadin *Symphonie*—formal sketch and notes. Abridged Sonata-Allegro form

	EXPOSITION				DEVELOPMENT	RECAPITULATION		
Measure	(1-23)	(24-39)	(40-55)	(56-77)	(78-136)	(137-152)	(153-168)	(169-200)
Themes[1]	PT	ST	CT	Codetta	Fragments of all themes	[No PT]	ST	CT Coda
Tonal (key) structure	F	C	C	C	Am and Dm alternating Cycle of 5ths C^7	F	F	F

The development section utilizes the ascending and descending quarter-note fragment from the PT and CT as well as the dotted eighth and sixteenth note rhythms.

m 14   m4, inversion   m4, neighboring—tone

see mm 20, 42, 50

The second part of the PT is developed at m 95. Fragments of the ST used with cycle of 5ths (mm 118-128).
Each formal section is clearly marked off by cadences and the key scheme follows the typical sonata-allegro pattern.

Psyché and Éros - formal sketch and notes

   The form of *Psyché and Éros* is not as readily discernible as the *Symphonie*. Certainly it has no "standard" design or pattern. Instead of a clear-cut sectional structure and key relationships, smooth transitions move the line from theme area to theme area and from key to key without marked separation—definitely without a feeling of periodicy and cadencing. Rather, the themes, and in a larger sense the form, are constructed of motives that build in sequential and dynamic waves from lesser to greater climax areas.

---

[1]PT: Principal or First Theme Group
ST: Subordinate or Second Theme Group
CT: Closing Theme Group

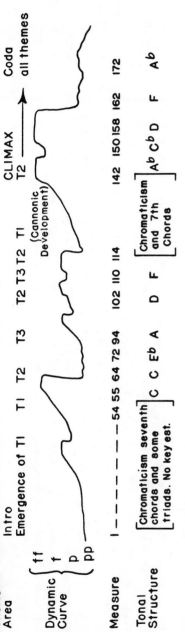

Thematically the germ motive of the work is found in mm 11-12 in the triadic idea.

This evolves with the melodic sigh (mm 13-14 & 15-16) into a climactic statement.

[2]T1: First Theme, T2: Second Theme, T3: Third Theme

[3]The tonal areas marked on the sketch often dissipate quickly through chromaticism, thus, do not function as tonal areas as in the *Symphonie.* However, the following list of major triads will provide the director with "land-mark" chords for tuning to improve overall intonation: m 34 A flat, 36 & 38 C flat, 49 F, 55 and 64 C, 72 E flat, 80 G flat, 84 & 94 A, 98 G flat, 102 D, 110 F, 117 & 119 A flat, 121 C flat, 139 C, 142 A flat, 150 C flat, 158 D, 162 F, 172 & 205 A flat.

The second theme embodies the triad and scale line of the first theme. (m 64-65).

The second part of the second theme is closely related rhythmically. The three-note scale line often widens to form a triad. (mm 80-81).

The third theme is related motivically to both other themes, although its statement by the bass instruments tends to associate it more closely with the opening theme (mm 94-97).

Thus, the music begins from a background of static, but expectant seventh chords. Although the composition is in A flat major, the opening is harmonically unclear. Gradually the first theme emerges with a climactic statement in C major (m 55). The second theme is stated *pianissimo* (beginning at m 64) in C major also. The second statement of this theme is intensified by an abrupt modulation by third relation to E flat major (m 72). The second part of the theme (beginning at m 80) also moves up another minor third to G flat. The third theme appears in A major (m 94), is repeated in G flat major, and followed by the second theme in D major. A canonic development of material from the first theme (m 118) gradually builds intensity through chromaticism, dissonance and dynamics to the climax of the composition (m 142). Here the second theme is stated *fortissimo* in A flat major. This is all the more dramatic since this is the first time the tonic has really become established. Although it was alluded to at the outset, it was strategically placed at the climax. This is quite a difference from the Classical tonal scheme. The second statement of the theme (m 150) is further intensified as before through a sudden modulation up a minor third to C flat major. The second section of the theme again moves up (m 158), this time to D major. The denouement comes quickly with the second part of the theme repeated softly in F major, beginning m 162. A coda which stresses the tonic key of A flat, begins at 172 and restates the themes. The composition ends softly as it began, but not with the same static quality. Instead dissonances push to the final A flat tonic triad.

Haydn London Symphony and Schubert Unfinished Symphony

Two musical examples in the same form will serve to illustrate the basic difference between classical and romantic even further. When contrasting these styles, one most often hears that the Classic emphasized "form" while the Romantic emphasized "content." However, all great or even good music has "content" and certainly has form. Rather than the usual "form" versus "content" dichotomy, these styles are best contrasted by noting the relative roles of musical "structure" and musical "materials." The Classicist concentrated upon structure—the manipulation of material. In a sense, material was immaterial because what was done with the material was most important. The Classicist built impressive forms (structures) from seemingly insignificant thematic material. On the other hand, the Romantics emphasized the direct sensuous impact of the materials as such—the sounds of chords (harmonic color), of melodies and theme (lyricism), of instrumentation (orchestral color), and of rhythms and dynamics for their immediate effect.

In the Haydn *London Symphony,* 1st Movement, *allegro,* the simple folk-like theme is presented at the outset (mm 17-36). The significance of this theme resides not in its "content" or its direct sensuous appeal, but in its potential. What can be done with the materials in the theme or what germinal potential do the fragments hold?

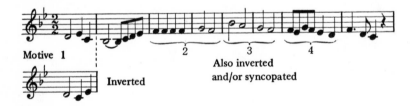

The theme fragments as numbered constitute the material from which the symphonic movement is constructed. Although outwardly in sonata-allegro form (Figure 10-3), this motivic manipulation and development constitutes the inner, evolving structure. The following listing is illustrative.[4]

Motive 1. –mm 32, 34, 65f, 86, 87, 208, 210, 247-255
Motive 1. Inverted–mm 54, 55, 104, 106, 108, 146f, 271, 273
Motive 2. –mm 50-52, 52-53, 124-144, 150-155, 159-192, 228-231 238-241, 277-280
Motive 3. –original and accompanying syncopations (all scale passages, and syncopations as mm 56, 61-62, 80, 92-4, 112-123, etc.)
Motive 4. –eighth-note figures constitute most transition materials and accompanying runs.

Schubert, as Beethoven, remained a Classicist in the sense that he retained the standard compositional forms. However, the influence of his times caused him to emphasize the lyrical and coloristic qualities above the manipulative. The "First Movement" of the *Unfinished Symphony* is in sonata-allegro form but offers a striking contrast to the *London Symphony.*

The introductory theme, stated in octaves by the bass instruments plays a functional structural role, unlike the "non-structural" slow introduction of the Haydn *London Symphony.* Schubert utilizes this theme almost exclusively in the development section. The principal and subordinant themes are lyrical in quality and stated fully. Fragmentation and development of these themes take place only in transitions and as closing material and not in the development section itself. Accompanying figures of sixteenth-notes and syncopations, however, are utilized in the development section. The tonal structure is unique also. Schubert used third relationship between the principal and subordinate themes. See Figure 10-4.

Although many developmental aspects are found, they are much more obvious than Haydn's. Schubert emphasizes his materials with much greater impact and length of composition. He

---

[4]The arranger simplified the rhythmic difficulties of the introduction by writing the original *adagio* (C, in 8) into 4/4 meter. For this reason, number every *two* measures. The allegro starts at m 17 in the transcription (at rehearsal number 4).

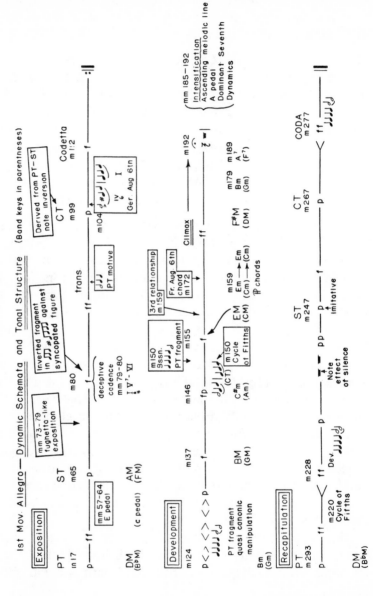

Haydn London Symphony (No. 104)

1st Mov. Allegro— Dynamic Schemata and Tonal Structure   (Band keys in parentheses)

Schubert Symphony No. 8, The Unfinished

1st Mov. Allegro moderato — Tonal Structure

Exposition

Intro. (1-8)	PT (9-37)	Trans. (38-43)	ST (44-61)	Trans. (63-72)	CT (73-93)	Codetta (94-110)
Cm	Cm		AbM		AbM [Dev. of ST ♫]	AbM → Cm [Dev. of ST ♪]

Development

(111-217)

Intro theme (115-134) Aug 6th	Inversion and original of Intro theme, Harmonic color [minor 9th chord] and Rhythmic drive thru diminution to climax (135-146)	Retrograde [♩♩♪ acc] (147-169)	Unison [Climax] (170-183)	Canon (184-193)	Retrograde and Dynamic Color [Sfz] (194-207)	Retransition [PT motive used] (208-217) Dom. V of Cm
Fm			Fm			

Recapitulation

PT (218-251)	Trans. (252-257)	ST (258-279)	Trans. (281-290)	CT (291-311)	Codetta (312-327)	Coda (Short Dev. of Intro. Theme) (328-368)
Cm		EbM		CM	CM	Cm

emphasizes the sounds of his melodies (lyricism); the sounds of the chords and dissonances (harmonic color); the sounds of the instruments playing the melodies, singly and in combination (orchestration). The sounds of rhythms (as cross rhythms and diminution of note values, mm. 135-146) and the sounds of *sforzando, crescendos* and *diminuendos* (dynamic shading). Schubert, in this sense, is a true Romanticist. The musical materials are savored and held as long as possible. This is music that is "being" as contrasted to the Classical evolutionary music, i.e., music that is "becoming."

Baroque compared to classical

The term "Baroque" was first used in a derogatory sense to designate the period of the "figured bass." It was derived from the Portugese "barocco," an irregular or imperfect pearl. By Classical standards, this period was indeed imperfect or irregular. However, this is because it was not judged by its own values.

High Baroque music is predominantly polyphonic in texture. Each voice was considered an independent line, but the polarity of the soprano and bass parts made them especially important. Imitation is the principal method of articulation. By contrast, polyphonic texture was reserved almost exclusively for development sections by Classical composers.

High baroque music is monothematic. That is, one theme is spun out sequentially or presented in imitation. This results in a well integrated composition in unified form, yet lacking in contrast by Classical standards. Phrase structure is often irregular with no marked feeling of cadence. Elision and overlapping cadences are used extensively for this effect. Strong cadences are reserved to define important formal divisions. The harmony is functional and key relationships are most essential to the overall form. The Baroque form did not depend upon thematic design as the Classical. Rather it consisted of essentially (1) a strong statement of key, (2) departure from that key, and (3) return to the key. The all-embracing concept gave coherence and meaning to all Baroque compositions. (This basic key relationship was also taken over by the Classicist.)

As the sonata-allegro was the important instrumental form of the Classical era, the *concerto grosso* was the instrumental form of the Baroque. The concerto principle contrasted a small group of instruments *(concertino)* with the remaining instruments in the orchestra *(ripieno)*. Often they also played together *(tutti)*. In a typical *concerto grosso,* the *tutti* presents the main theme in the tonic key. The movement from then on consists of alternations of the *concertino* and *ripieno* parts. The return of the theme in the *ripieno* is called the *ritornello.* Contrast is achieved by the contrasting sonority of the small and large groups. In each section the theme is treated by sequence or imitation.

Figure 10-5 provides a comprehensive comparison of a Handel *Concerto Grosso* and the *Military Symphony in F* by Gossec.

Figure 10-5

Concerto Grosso, 1st Mvt.	Military Symphony, 1st Mvt.

MELODY

1. Theme stated at outset and repeated at the octave, followed by a sequential spinning out (mm 5-7 **and** mm 9-13).	1. Short symmetrical phrases. Dialogue (action-reaction) phraseology. See especially mm 15-20.

HARMONY

1. Triads and seventh chords.	1. Triads and seventh chords.
2. Many elided cadences (mm 23,45, 65, and 93).	2. Definite cadences at all phrase endings and formal divisions.
3 Generally fast harmonic rhythm (harmonies change quickly).	3. Generally slow harmonic rhythm.
4. Bass line should be emphasized as an important contributing part to the texture.	4. Bass line often merely supports the harmonic structure, e.g., mm 15-27 and mm 52-59.

TEMPO

1. *Allegro*, but not too fast. An on-going drive necessary.	1. *Allegro maestoso* should move with well articulated and even rhythms. The back and forth phrase structure and scale passages should not be allowed to rush.

TEXTURE

1. Both polyphonic and homophonic texture found. The continuo parts are often imitative. (The third movement is polyphonic—a fugal texture predominates throughout.)	1. Homophonic, although occasional movements of inner and bass lines suggest polyphony.

TRILLS

1. Idiomatically, trills are approached from above in Baroque style.

1. Trills often approached from above in Classical style, although it was the period of change (mm 5-8 of third movement).

ORCHESTRATION

1. Full band *(ripieno)* against solo group *(concertino)*.

1. More color exploitation, especially in the final movement. Note oboe duet, mm 9-10 and use of high woodwind m 32, m 34 etc.

DYNAMICS

1. "Terrace" dynamics. Contrasts of louds and softs often created by the number of instruments playing.

1. *Crescendos, diminuendos, sforzandos,* and other shadings indicated, in addition to loud versus soft phraseology.

ARTICULATION

1. Heavy with full note values, but on-going drive and flow of beat maintained.

1. Light, clear, well articulated.

FORM

I Allegro
II Largo
III Allegro

I Allegro Maestoso
II Larghetto
III Allegro

FORMAL ANALYSIS

Concerto Grosso,   First Movement

Tutti (mm 1-18):   (*Ripieno* plus *concertino*) introduces the main theme, which sounds similar to the "Hallelujah Chorus," in the key of C major. It is treated sequentially through the dominant G and back again to C.

Concertino (mm 19-22):   flute figurations based upon theme.

Ripieno (mm 23-24):   short *ritornello* modulating to G.

Concertino (mm 25-30):   again figurations based upon theme.

Ripieno (mm 31-32):   short *ritornello.*

Concertino (mm 33-45):   long passage typical of idiomatic writing for the solo instruments. Features displays of technique.

Ripieno (mm 45-50):   sequential melody line, cadencing in G.

(mm 51-72):   continued alteration of *continuo* and *ripieno* moving through E minor.

Tutti (mm 73-end):   final *ritornello* in C, which is similar to the first theme statement but often changing sonority between *tutti, ripieno,* and *concertino.*

Second Movement

This movement is in the relative minor, and is typical of many Baroque slow movements. The long, flowing line of Flute I moves from beginning to end with no definite break, although several strong cadences appear (m3 in A minor, m 8 in D minor and m 11 in A minor). These cadences must be treated as elisions. Note also the many sequences (mm 3 and 4, m 8) that contribute to the long spun-out quality of the movement. The effect of the half cadence at the end helps to finalize the long line, yet anticipate the final movement. (The contrast with the "Second Movement" of the *Military Symphony* is most striking.) The dotted sixteenth and thirty-second note rhythm serves as a unifying force. Play *legato,* in rhythm, with emphasis upon the dotted note.

Third Movement

The final movement begins with the theme stated as a fugal exposition, followed by a *tutti* (mm 9-16) in the key of C. The *concertino* continues the polyphonic texture based upon the fugal countersubject (mm 16-33), and the *ripieno* cadences in G (m 40). *Concertino, tutti,* and *ripieno* sections alternate, moving through the keys of A minor and E minor. Both imitative writing and long sequential phrases are found. The final *ritornello* (m 89) receives further *tutti* development before reaching a culminating *adagio* cadence. In all three movements, rhythmic accuracy and careful balance of lines is necessary.[5]

Military Symphony First Movement

The movement is sectional with frequent divisive cadences. It is set in three parts and suggests a sonata-allegro structure on a miniature scale.

	EXPOSITION				DEVELOPMENT	RECAPITULATION		
Theme Groups	PT	ST	CT	Codetta	‖: Based upon several fragments of themes	PT	[No CT ST]	Coda :‖
Tonal Structure	F	C	C	C	C	F	F	F
Measure	(1-10)(11-14)(15-22)(23-27)				(28-39)	(40-47)	(48-53)	(54-59)

---

[5] The Vivaldi *Concerto for Two Trumpets* can be substituted as a Baroque example. The arrangement is in B flat instead of C. The accompaniment part is much easier, especially if the repeated sixteenth-notes are changed to eighths where necessary. The trumpet parts require good players, however. Key relationships remain quite close, basically tonic and dominant. Sequential and canonic (imitative) treatment are quite evident.

The style throughout should be very light and articulated in contrast to the heavier Baroque. Never get a "tut-tut" type of articulation, however. Strive to think of a bouncing *spiccato* bowing as a guide. Accents also should be approached as emphasis, never a literal explosive or labored force of tone. Never clip off a final phrase note. Even if it is marked staccato or marcato it must be rounded off (♩ = ◻ , never ◻ "tut"). See the last note (m 27) and all similar places. Often students play this as a harsh attack followed by a forced release with no tone in between.

There is a similar problem with the feminine cadences (mm 15-18). In each measure, the dissonance (dominant seventh chord) occurs on a strong beat and the consonance (tonic chord) resolves on a weak beat. The parts are marked with an accent on the half note which by length should receive emphasis anyway. Yet students have a tendency to misinterpret the figure. They inevitably play [notation] instead of, [notation] (stress to release).[6]

Balance and intonation of chords is essential. The tempo must not rush. All sixteenth-note runs must be even. Dynamics must be followed carefully but *fortes* never overblown.

Second Movement

The form is ternary.

Design	A		B(based upon A)		A	
	a	a'			a	a'
Tonal Structure	F: I--V⁷I--V⁷I		IV-I-V²I, IV-I		F: I--V⁷I--V⁷I	
			C: IV-V²I---V²I			
			c pedal			
Measure	1 - - - - 4		5 - - - - - - - - 12		13 - - - - - 16	

[6]Examples of this can be found throughout the standard band literature. The opening phrase endings of the Holst *Second Suite in F* come to mind since this was a required festival number recently. Only one band of the ten heard played this cadential figure correctly.

The first and last sections are comprised of identical parallel periods. The middle section (beginning m 5) is based upon the thematic material from the first section that modulates to the dominant key of C. Motives are developed, and dynamics and cross rhythms are utilized to intensify the climax at the *fermata*. The dialogue type of phrasing is much in evidence. Note how this construction is antithetical to the slow movement of the *Concerto Grosso*.

Third Movement

This movement is constructed of short, seemingly unrelated phrases, similar to some movements by Mozart. However, compare the relationship of mm 11-16 with mm 25-30, and mm 5-9 with 39-41. There is also a similar melodic shape in mm 1-4 and mm 31-32.

shape

The tonal scheme is very simple, staying close to tonic and dominant. The first section cadences in the dominant (m 20). The tonic key is quickly restated, however (m 25).

Polyphonic texture appears briefly in this predominantly homophonic setting. It is most notable as an intensification of the final four bars where the important themes are sounded simultaneously.

The Classical style exemplified in the *Military Symphony* illustrates a light delicate, refined quality that may lack profoundness, but possesses clarity. It should be performed with perfect control, precision and restraint—a polished gem of music, not an irregular pearl.

11

How to Teach Musicianship
Through Interpreting
the Score

The band director is responsible for the interpretation of the music his band plays. Yet, students can learn about it and contribute to it. Obviously a vote cannot be taken to decide the interpretation of each phrase during a concert. However, much rehearsal time can be saved if students understand and respond to the expressive symbols of music. They will become more musically mature and independent if they learn the "how and why" of musical expression and interpretation.

This chapter investigates the two important "indicators" of interpretation—(1) expression marks, and (2) musical structure. Specific methods are suggested to teach them to students.

EXPRESSION MARKS

Expression marks are the added written directions in the music that guide the performance. Composers began using the more or less universal system of Italian words, abbreviations and signs in the Eighteenth Century to indicate more effectively the desired interpretation of their music. In the course of musical practice since that time, composers, arrangers and editors have used these designations with greater frequency and care.

Teach your students that expression marks deal with the three major elements of expression over which the performer has the most control—(1) dynamics, (2) tempo, and (3) style or mood. A student study chart like Figure 11-1 should be distributed to help each student learn the expression marks that you feel are the most important.

Figure 11-1

STUDENT STUDY SHEET

Expressions Marks

Expression marks deal with the three major elements of expression over which the performer has the most direct, individual control: dynamics, tempo, and style or mood.

I. Dynamics
    A. Markings that indicate the degree of intensity from soft to loud.
        1. *Pianissimo* (pp)—very softly
        2. *Piano* (p)—softly
        3. *Mezzo-piano* (mp)—moderately softly
        4. *Mezzo-forte* (mf)—moderately loudly
        5. *Forte* (f)—loudly
        6. *Fortissimo* (ff)—very loudly
    B. Markings for gradual changes in dynamics.
        1. *Crescendo (cresc.* or◁)—gradually increasing
        2. *Diminuendo (dim.* or▷)—gradually diminishing volume or intensity
        3. *Morendo*—dying away
    C. Markings that indicate abrupt dynamic changes or accents.
        1. *Forte-piano* (fp)—attack the note strongly but diminish instantly
        2. *Sforzando* (sfz)—play with force or emphasis

II. Tempo
    A. Markings that designate the relative speed of the beat.
        1. *Largo*—the slowest tempo in music
        2. *Grave*—heavy, slow
        3. *Lento*—slow
        4. *Adagio*—slowly, leisurely
        5. *Andante*—moderately slow, flowing
        6. *Moderato*—moderately
        7. *Allegretto*—moderately fast
        8. *Allegro*—quick, lively
        9. *Vivace*—animated, very quick
      10. *Presto*—fast
    B. Metronome markings for exact tempo indications
        1. ♩ = 100
        2. ♪ = 120
    C. Markings that indicate tempo changes
        1. *Accelerando (accel.)*—accelerating, gradually increasing tempo
        2. *Ritardando (ritard.)*—gradually slowing tempo
        3. *Ritenuto (rit.)*—holding back; abruptly slowing tempo
        4. *Rallentando (rall.)*—gradually slowing tempo, usually at the end of a section or composition
        5. *Stringendo (string.)*—hastening
        6. *Allargando (allarg.)*—broaden
        7. *Piu mosso*—more movement
        8. *Meno mosso*—less movement
        9. *A tempo*)return to original tempo
    D. Markings for a tempo pause at climactic notes.
        1. *Fermata* (⌢)—a hold
        2. *Tenuto* (ten.)—sustain for emphasis; an agogic accent

III. Style or Mood
    A. Markings used to indicate general style
        1. *Legato* (⌢)(—)—smooth, connected style
        2. *Staccato* (·)—light, separated style
        3. *Marcato* (>)—heavy, separated style
    B. Some markings used to designate more specific style and mood.
        1. *Agitato*—agitated
        2. *Animato*—with spirit; animated

    3. *Appassionato*—with intense emotion and feeling
    4. *Cantabile*—in a singing style
    5. *Con brio*—with spirit, dash, vigor
    6. *Con fuoco*—with fire
    7. *Dolce*—sweetly
    8. *Grandioso*—with grandeur; noble
    9. *Grazioso*—graceful style
  10. *Maestoso*—majestically
  11. *Pesante*—heavily
  12. *Sotto voce*—subdued voice

C. Some tempo markings that also connote style and mood.
    1. *Andante*—flowing style
    2. *Allegretto*—light and cheerful
    3. *Allegro spirito*—quick with spirit
    4. *Grave*—slow and solemn movement
    5. *Largo*—slow and stately movement
    6. *Alla marcia*—in march tempo

Rehearsal follow-up

The study sheet is the initial step. The director must now concentrate upon expression marks in the music being performed. He must require students to read carefully "around the notes" to achieve the interpretation as indicated. The following outline includes pitfalls that must be avoided.

Dynamics. Work for a full range of dynamics and away from the bland *mezzo-forte* sound. On the other hand guard against the harsh, over-blown *forte* and the anemic, fuzzy or breathy *piano.* All tones need breath support! This includes maintaining tones at full volume. Final tones, especially, tend to fade away or "fizzle out."

To force the band to utilize the full five or six-degree volume spectrum, numbers can be assigned to each level. Then practice *crescendos* and *diminuendos.*

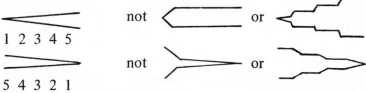

1 2 3 4 5

5 4 3 2 1

Another technique is to ask the band to play a *fortissimo,* then a *forte,* then a *mezzo-forte,* etc., until a *pianissimo* is reached. It is my experience that it ends up very soft. Again make sure that every *pianissimo* is supported and balanced. Both vertical (chordal) and linear (melodic) balance depend upon careful dynamic control.

Tempo. Work for a steady pulse—no rushing or dragging. Students should feel the beat "swing." (See Chapter 3.)

Style or Mood. Reference has been made to the basic styles of music and how they can be taught. Many other terms have been used by composers to designate the specific styles or moods in their compositions. These "word pictures" offer further clues to the desired performance. The performer must try to capture and "project" this mood in performance.

Many Romantic and Contemporary scores abound with stylistic expression indications. Have your students attempt to define the terms in such a work. The Persichetti *Symphony for Band* is a real challenge. It soon becomes evident that a pocket music dictionary is a must for all serious students (and directors), for it is impossible to memorize all of the different terms in use today.

Limitations of Expression Marks. All of the above-mentioned expression marks have certain limitations. (1) They indicate *what* to do but they do not tell *why.* (2) Even though editors and arrangers have supplied even more expression marks than composers in an effort to help students toward more expressive playing, everything cannot possibly be written into the score and parts. (3) Expression marks, themselves, do not encompass every aspect of musical expression. In the next section, interpretation is sought in the musical structure and phrase.

MUSICAL STRUCTURE AND INTERPRETATION

Since expression marks are singularly insufficient to explain musical interpretation, one further step must be taken to relate expression to musical structure, phrasing and "line." The theory of expression based upon intensity and movement can be explained to your group as background to a unit upon phrasing.

The nature of musical expression

In recent times, aestheticians, psychologists and educators have developed and expanded the basic ideas long held or instinctively felt by musicians—that intensity and motion are central to musical meaning, expression and interpretation. In general, this theory postulates that music is significant or expressive because the forms of music are similar to the forms of human feeling. The rationale is easy to follow: All that we experience is accompanied by some degree of feeling. Furthermore, the pattern or structure of feeling is cyclic, fluctuating between tension and the resolution of tension. We all have our ups and downs, frustrations and successes, disappointments and windfalls, good days and bad days.

Similarly, music can be defined as perceived tonal movement through patterns of tensions and resolutions. Or, to paraphrase Hanslick, music presents forms of intensity to release in tonal motion. These patterns are isomorphic to the life of human feeling. Thus, music's movement through patterns of intensity to release is expressive of man's experience through actual psychological and physiological tensions and resolutions. Rise-fall, struggle-fulfillment, anticipation-goal attainment, movement-repose, tension-resolution are all antithetical terms used to describe what happens in both music and life.

The performer must be aware, then, that any element of music that contributes to its tension and motion is expressive. Stating it as simply as possible, interpretation and expression depend upon the broader aspects of phrase line. The "line" of music moves through the phrase to cadence in a rise-fall, intensity-release manner. This rise or tension is usually brought about by a melodic rise, *crescendo,* slight *accelerando,* dissonance, harmonic progression and drive, and/or a *tenuto* at the phrase climax. The falling away or release of intensity is brought about by melodic fall, *diminuendo,* slight *ritardando,* and/or cadence and consonance. The formal design also has these elements of tension-contrast in the statement-departure-restatement of musical form (the A B A pattern in all of its infinite varieties). This intensity-release pattern of music is the fundamental structure from which all interpretation and musical expression springs.

In the next section, a step by step procedure is given for the presentation of phrasing and line through specific music being performed.

Teaching phrase and line

Almost any slow, sustained, *legato* melody is appropriate for teaching phrasing. Several were used in earlier chapters to illustrate melody and harmony. Four pieces are used in this discussion: Grainger, *Ye Banks and Braes O' Bonnie Doon* and the second movements from Vaughan Williams *English Folk Song Suite,* Holst *Second Suite,* and Grainger *Lincolnshire Posey.* Teach your students from the music using the following outline as a guide.

I   Principles of line—tonal movement through patterns of tensions and resolutions—within the phrase.

    A. The usual shape of a phrase is a melodic rise-fall curve. Intensity is achieved in ascent, release in descent.

Ex. 11—1   "Song Without Words"   from *Second Suite*
                  by Gustav Holst

© Copyright 1922 by Boosey & Company Limited. Renewed 1949
Used by permission of Boosey & Hawkes Inc.

The phrase arch can be diagrammed as follows:

Have your students physically get the feel of the upward surge and downward release. It forms the basis of all to follow.

    B. Dynamically, a slight *crescendo* and *diminuendo* follow the rise-fall curve, heightening the intensity and release.

Ex. 11—2   "Song Without Words" from *Second Suite*
                  by Gustav Holst

© Copyright 1922 by Boosey & Company Limited. Renewed 1949
Used by permission of Boosey & Hawkes Inc.

Several other points can be brought out by the director concerning dynamic and agogic accents—certain notes receive special emphasis.

    1. You can think of a melody as a hierarchy of notes (generals, colonels, etc., down to privates). Less im-

portant notes receive less emphasis and usually lead to more important notes. Fast, technical passages are easier to perform when you locate the important points for which to aim.

2. Certain melodic tones demand more emphasis because of their place in the tonal structure. Some are "active" or "stress" tones which seek resolution. They move to "passive" or "rest" tones. Teach scale tendencies as, for example, the upward pull of the leading tone to tonic. Have students get the physical feel for these stresses as they perform.

3. Unexpected, out of key, or modulating tones are tension producing and need more emphasis.

4. Note lengths provide a cue for emphasis. Generally, the longer the note, the more emphasis it receives.

5. It is most important to locate and give special emphasis to the climax (often the high point) of all phrases and melodies.

Ex. 11–3 "Song Without Words" from *Second Suite*
         by Gustav Holst

© Copyright 1922 by Boosey & Company Limited. Renewed 1949
Used by permission of Boosey & Hawkes Inc. (mm 15–18)

Climax

6. Repeated tones will usually *crescendo* to give the feeling of intensity and movement.

7. Similarly, long, sustained tones will usually *crescendo* to heighten the feeling of intensity and movement.

8. Musical tone, itself, can be intensified without discernable volume change. This is often achieved by means of vibrato, although clarinetists and horn players must find other ways.

C. A rhythmic drive to cadence follows the melodic rise-fall curve. This towardness or progression is another important basis for the shape of the phrase. Furthermore, locating cadences—the points of musical rest or release—is the best method of identifying cadences.

1. Generally, the phrase moves in an almost imperceptible *accelerando* and *ritardando* that follows the melodic rise-fall curve, heightening the intensity and release.

Ex, 11—4 *Ye Banks & Braes O' Bonnie Doon*
by Percy Grainger

© Copyright 1949 by G.Schirmer Inc. Used by permission.

Slight *accel.* (intensify tempo)   *rit.*

2. Another type of phrase movement requires a slackening of time within the phrase or a *tenuto,* with a subsequent "catching up" to the original tempo. Intensity is achieved by a slight *ritenuto.* A wide intervallic leap is usually indicative of this phrase movement.

Ex. 11—5 "Intermezzo" from *English Folk Song Suite*
by Vaughan Williams

©Copyright 1924 by Boosey & Company Limited. Renewed 1951
Used by permission of Boosey & Hawkes Inc.

(*slight rit.*)   (*accel.*)   (*rit.*)

3. Both types of phrase movement are found in this melody.

Ex. 11—6 "Intermezzo" from *English Folk Song Suite*
by Vaughan Williams

© Copyright 1924 by Boosey & Company Limited. Renewed 1951
Used by permission of Boosey & Hawkes Inc.

In general, phrases move to a culminating point of intensity and then to a confirming close. Have your students feel the progression as a wave of tension moving to relaxation. Remember, however, that execution of phrase movement does not imply distortion of the basic pulse. The intensity is built within the framework of the beat.

D. Rhythmic devices are also used to create intensity and phrase movement.

   1. Decreasing note values drive and intensify.

Ex. 11–7 *Ye Bank & Braes O' Bonnie Doon*
      by Percy Grainger
© Copyright 1949 by G.Schirmer Inc. Used by permission.

   2. Extended rhythmic and motivic repetition creates intensity.

   3. Heavy rhythm tends to intensify more than light rhythm. However, accented weak beats create more intensity than accented strong beats.

   4. Irregular rhythm and meter create more intensity than regular. Syncopation and polymeter are good examples.

E. Intensity is heightened most by dissonance or dischord. Release is attained in resolution to consonance.

   1. An authentic cadence is, itself, a dissonance to consonance.

   Ex. 11–8

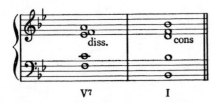

   2. Dissonance demands movement and seeks resolution.

Note the A flat grinding against the A natural (count 1); the D flat against the D natural, and the A flat against the G natural (count 3).

Ex. 11–9 "Second Movement" from *Lincolnshire Posey*
         by Percy Grainger

II Principles of line—tonal movement through patterns of tensions and resolutions—within the total composition.

   Phrases and themes are progressions that move to other phrases or sections in the total composition. In the A B A form, the departure or digression creates intensity, the restatement brings release. Look at the complete first statement of the Grainger setting of *Ye Banks and Braes O' Bonnie Doon*.

Ex. 11–10 *Ye Banks & Braes O' Bonnie Doon*
          by Percy Grainger

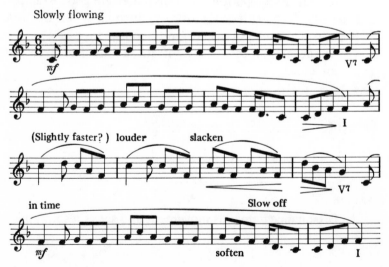

The dynamics, phrasing, tempo and performance suggestions were all inserted by Grainger. You can hardly miss with this number as a technically easy, yet expressively effective band arrangement.

It is a simple a a b a form, consisting of a parallel period and a contrasting period. The first phrase ends on a half cadence, the dominant-seventh chord. A slight *ritardando* would be appropriate here after the phrase was pushed through to cadence. The second phrase can be ritarded a little more after it too has been pushed through to the tonic cadence. However, the big *ritardando* must be reserved for the end.

The contrasting "b" section is emphasized by a change in dynamics and a suggested (but not to be overdone) tempo change. I interpret the "question mark" inserted by Grainger as a warning that all shadings should be subtle, almost imperceptible modifications that must never be perceived as distortions of the music. The climax occurs on the D (m12). The contrast has further tensional significance for it too ends on a dominant-seventh chord that "demands" a restatement of the "a" theme.

Look again at the "Largo" theme from Dvorak's *New World Symphony*. The climax comes in the intensification of the final "a," rather than in the contrasting "b" section. (See Chapter 4.) The "Song Without Words" by Holst also has some expressive "twists" within the small a a b a form.

Ex. 11–11 "Song Without Words" from *Second Suite*
by Gustav Holst

The first phrase moves as expected with a written agogic accent at the high point of the phrase and a weak cadence created by a minor seventh instead of a dominant-seventh chord. This phrase is intensified to the E flat and released at the cadence. The second phrase has an unexpected turn when the intensity is further elevated to the melodic "f" and a major chord on the subdominant (B flat). The contrasting section (b) is more active harmonically and concludes with a most effective suspension on the minor, half cadence. This creates added intensity for the restatement. The climax of the final phrase is also the climax of the song. It is approached in an ascending scale-wise progression in a freed *(ad libitum)* rhythm indicated by the composer. The composer uses a *fermata* to emphasize the climax note. If *fermati* are understood as the climactic and highly tensional focal points of the musical line, their execution will become more meaningful and more easily apprehended by performers.

One final example, the second movement of Grainger's *Lincolnshire Posey,* is a fine study in phrasing and climax. The theme is a lovely melody with a climactic apex in the fifth measure. The complete movement consists of four statements of the theme, each intensified more than the one before. Intensity is achieved through instrumentation, dynamics, and particularly dissonance. Note, for example, the long, sustained F flat major-seventh chord from measures seventeen through twenty-four. Seventh chords are used effectively throughout. The climax of the movement occurs at m34 where A flat grinds against A natural, and D flat against D natural at *fortissimo* volume.

To interpret, then, your students must move the on-going line of music to the cadential points of repose. Students and director must answer such questions as "Where is the music going?" "Where does it lead?" And, of course, "How does it get there?" What "turns of phrase," what unexpected, tensional notes affect its course? Philip Farkas explains these intensity points in the following way:

> There is, in a musical phrase, almost always one or more "pivot" notes, around which the phrase seems to center. I call them pivot notes because, as the phrase leads to such

a note, it seems to require more and more intensity (like traveling up a hill) until this note is reached, at which point the direction pivots and a feeling of relaxation appears. . .

This pivot point is an intangible thing and at times may cover more than one note. It may be in the lower notes of a phrase, in which case the intensity must continue to increase toward it even though the notes progress in a downward direction. This is contrary to the common, but mistaken belief of many students, who always like to make crescendos on ascending passages and diminuendos on the way down. . . .[1]

---

[1] Philip Farkas, *The Art of French Horn Playing*, (Evanston, Illinois: Summy-Birchard, 1956), p. 55.

12

How to Develop Musical Discrimination in the Student

The competent band director has earned the respect of his students. This is the basis for his musical leadership. He is well liked, admired, respected, and he influences the standards of the students in his groups. This may be an unconscious process, but it operates nonetheless. He expects his students to have high performance standards. When he is on the podium, he requires his students to give their all to achieve a high level of performance, and exerts his "influence" in every way to insure this. How can the conductor further influence the standards of students in all areas of value judgment in music?

In this chapter, suggestions are made to develop a high level of discrimination in band students. Students are helped to answer these questions: What is good performance? What is good style? What is good music?

JUDGING PERFORMANCE

The director's first step is to foster an awareness of the elements of good performance. The adjudicators comment sheet provides an excellent medium through which to begin, especially if your group participates in competition festivals. However, whether you participate or not, the elements of performance are the same. For handy reference, put a large copy of the adjudication items on the front wall so that it faces the students.

Figure 12-1

ADJUDICATORS COMMENT SHEET

TONE (beauty, blend, control)
INTONATION (chords, melodic line, tutti)
TECHNIQUE (articulation, facility, precision, rhythm)
BALANCE (ensemble, sectional)
INTERPRETATION (expression, phrasing, style, tempo)
MUSICAL EFFECT (artistry, fluency)
OTHER FACTORS (choice of music, instrumentation, discipline, ap-
    pearance)

The adjudicators form represents a rational attempt to isolate the critical elements of performance so they can be evaluated. The meaning of each category should be brought out in rehearsal and referred to each time it is appropriate. These questions are appropriate.

Tone

1. Is the quality characteristic of the instrument?
2. Is the problem the reed, mouthpiece, embouchure, or breath control?
3. Is the tone consistent throughout the registers?
4. Is the tone controlled at all dynamic levels and consistent from attack to release?
5. Are some instruments not blending with the group? Sticking out? Overblowing?

Intonation

1. Are sections in tune with other sections and the band as a whole?

2. Are individuals in tune with their section and with the band as a whole?
3. Are individuals in tune with themselves? What are the out-of-tune notes? (Check especially the high woodwinds.)

Technique

1. Are all notes and rhythms played correctly?
2. Are runs even?
3. Is the articulation followed as marked in the score?
4. Are attacks and releases precise?

Balance

1. Are parts balanced in the section or do first parts predominate?
2. Are sections balanced or do certain "strong" sections predominate in the ensemble?
3. Are the "highs" predominating?
4. Is the middle too heavy and muddy?

Interpretation

1. Are dynamic markings carefully followed?
2. Are the phrases "led" to cadence and artfully rounded off?
3. Are all players playing the same style?
4. Are all players playing the correct style?
5. Is the tempo steady (not rushing or dragging)?
6. Is the tempo appropriate for the music?

Musical effect

1. Is the performance artistic?
2. Is the performance vital and convincing?
3. Does the total performance "come off"?

Other factors

1. Are the players attentive?
2. Do they sit up?
3. Are they really trying?
4. Do they seem to be enjoying what they are doing?

Students love to criticize the performances of others, especially of other "competing" performing groups. Malicious, unconstructive and noneducative criticism should not be condoned. Students should be encouraged to be critical listeners and evaluate performances as an adjudicator would evaluate them. Usually students have difficulty pin-pointing problems of performance unless they hear obvious "goofs" of an individual or section. Instead of undirected "cutting," give them copies of the adjudicators form or check lists as Figure 11-2 and let them be real critics. Here are several ways to direct student attention to actual problems of performance.

1. Give one (or more students) a condensed score and an adjudicators form. Charge him with the task of adjudicating his band in a rehearsal. Different students can be chosen each day.

2. Have students listen to ensembles with score and adjudicators form to help the ensembles prepare for festivals.

3. Have your students evaluate other groups with adjudicators forms as part of their participation in music festivals. This will force them to listen carefully to other groups and encourage the desired positive attitude of competition festival evaluation. A certain number of forms can be distributed to each student (for example, three). These can be collected at the end of the day.

Figure 12-2 is a check list that has been developed for student use. It is easier than the standard adjudicators form, and provides a good introduction to the standard form.

Figure 12-2

STUDENT'S PERFORMANCE AND REHEARSAL EVALUATION FORM

Indicate by measure number the instrument or section having the problem.

Good	Adequate	Poor	
___	___	___	**INTONATION**
			Who is out of tune? ___
			Sharp? ___
			Flat? ___
___	___	___	**TONE QUALITY**
			Characteristic Tone?
			Individual ___
			Section ___

Good   Adequate   Poor

_____   _____   _____   BALANCE

Who is "sticking out"? _____
What section is too loud? _____
What section is too soft? _____
Do you hear all important lines? _____

_____   _____   _____   WRONG NOTES

Who played wrong notes? _____
What was the error? _____
   Out of key? _____
   Out of rhythm? _____
   Incorrect fingerings? _____
   Lack of technique? _____
Need individual practice? _____

_____   _____   _____   PRECISION

Playing together? _____
Attacks? _____
Releases? _____
Articulation? _____
   Markings followed? _____
   Style achieved? _____
Runs even? _____

_____   _____   _____   TEMPO

Rushing? _____
Dragging? _____
Appropriate? _____

_____   _____   _____   DYNAMICS

Dynamic marking followed? _____
Dynamic levels achieved? _____
Subtle shadings achieved? _____

_____   _____   _____   PHRASING

Music flows? _____
Phrasing achieved? _____
Phrase "chopped up"? _____

GENERAL COMMENTS:

_____   _____   _____

JUDGING INTERPRETATION OF HISTORICAL STYLES

In addition to those general problems that constitute minimal standards for acceptable performance, students should be able to discriminate the performance practices of the major historical periods. (See Chapter 8.) To develop discrimination, have one or more students listen to the band at each rehearsal to check upon interpretation. They can use a checklist similar to the Style Chart (Figure 12-3). This sheet can be used at festivals and other performances as well.

Figure 12-3

STUDENT STYLE CHART—PERFORMANCE PRACTICE

BAROQUE

Yes	No	
____	____	Tone: full, heavy, block _____
____	____	Articulation: heavy with full note values _____
		slight separation of longer tones _____
		shorter tones, heavy and connected _____
____	____	Dynamics: terraced _____
____	____	Balance: equal (balanced) lines in counterpoint _____
		emphasis upon melody and bass in
		homophonic texture _____
____	____	Rhythm and Tempo: driving, steady _____
		beat emphasized _____
		dotted figures _____
____	____	Ornamentation: correctly executed _____
		trills even, initiated from trill note __
		trills ended with a turn _____

CLASSICAL

Yes	No	
____	____	Tone: light, pure, restrained, straight _____
____	____	Articulation: light, crisp, precise, accurate _____
		staccato notes lightened _____
		final notes never clipped _____
		feminine cadence, heavy-light _____
____	____	Dynamics: controlled, carefully played _____
		accents (emphasis), one degree louder __
____	____	Rhythm and Tempo: strict, light _____
		well-articulated _____

ROMANTIC

Yes	No		
——	——	Tone: full, big, warm _____	
		vibrato used appropriately to intensify ____	
——	——	Articulation: heavy, intense _____	
		follow markings _____	
——	——	Dynamics: wide range _____	
		long *crescendos* gradually fed _____	
		markings followed _____	
——	——	Phrasing: long phrases carried through _____	
		expressive shadings followed _____	
——	——	Rhythm and Tempo: expressive use of rubato _____	

CONTEMPORARY

Yes	No	
——	——	Tone: characteristic, clear, pure _____
——	——	Articulation: played exactly as marked _____
——	——	Dynamics: played exactly as marked _____
——	——	Balance: important lines predominate _____
		equal lines in linear texture _____
——	——	Rhythm and Tempo: steady, accurate _____
		jazz rhythms adjusted _____

VALUE JUDGMENTS OF MUSIC

There are no absolute values in music or objective criteria to judge given compositions. Yet, band directors make frequent judgments about the worth of music as part of their day by day functioning. "This work is great!" "I think this arrangement is much better than the other." "We have read through that composition and it stinks."

What are the bases of our choices? Music by the so-called great composers is always safe to use. We are influenced by the composer's reputation and the comments of critics, authorities and other band directors. We also have a "feel" for what we like based upon our background, musical experience and previous likes. Our ability to understand or "feel at home" with a certain style influences our choices. A director who "feels" phrases and can "pull a line" often prefers Romantic music; while a director who approaches music more intellectually prefers Classical or Contemporary music. He can approach these scores more objectively to achieve his musical ends. For teaching purposes, however, directors should use a wide range of styles. Students must learn about all types of music because training and experience are the most important factors in musical preference.

The director is a musical leader in the community. If he has done his "PR" work well, he has sold himself and his program. He cannot tell his students what to like, but he is in a good position to influence them.

Understanding is the key. The student must know enough about the music to be in a position to make a value judgment. In this sense, appreciation means understanding. Explain to the students that they can appreciate something and still not like it. For example, a person may understand the game of basketball well, and really "appreciate" what the professional basketball players can do. Yet, he may prefer professional football and never attend or follow basketball games.

In a similar way, students must study a complex, serious work of music to understand it. Often a great piece of music is difficult to get to know. It makes no sense. The story of the old Englishman at his first American football game illustrates this well. His reaction included boredom and comments something like these: "What a barbaric thing. We got rid of men in armor and jousting after the Middle Ages. Those men line up, bump heads together, and chase up and down the field after that extraordinary ball. It is not even round!" He should learn the rules.

Band students should learn the rules, too. A student's first reaction to a fugue is often one of boredom. A fugue is usually hard to put together in rehearsal. The independent lines require concentration and good reading ability on the part of each student—and, of course, one added difficulty—counting rests. However, after learning the "rules" of the form, students can listen to the work unfold and to their part in relation to the total complexity.

Peer culture music

Peer pressures strongly influence teenagers' musical choices. They have "their" music and sometimes resent this music being "used" in the school. Pop music also appeals because it expresses teenage experience better than the complex works of serious music. It is "relevant" to the age. By and large, pop music can be classified as immature, adolescent art. It is comparable to popcorn, third-rate drive-in movies, and comic books.

I have heard students argue that much of their music has serious intent, that it has social significance, and that it expresses deep meaning. This is often "verbally" true. However, a serious message carried by a lyric has nothing to do with musical quality. The music must stand on its own merits. Band music has no lyric. The music, itself, must carry the weight.

Without education, then, the students' musical preferences are limited to the cliché, stereotype formulae that are typical of most popular music.

Band transcriptions

Much heat has been generated for years in the musical world over the value of transcriptions of orchestral and organ music for band. Serious scholars (and musicologists) consider this practice a perversion of the original, a poor imitation and certainly no substitute. In a similar vein, many modern band directors advocate the exclusive use of original works for band.

While these arguments contain much academic and artistic merit, transcriptions in a very practical sense make much great music available to the band and to the bands' audiences. While there are many excellent original works for the modern band that should be used extensively, their exclusive use would severely limit the band repertory. Transcriptions must be used in order to study all of the historical styles adequately.

Criteria for evaluating band music

Several criteria can be used to help students make value judgments about the music they play. Criteria include (1) complexity and challenge, (2) lasting interest and value, (3) technical achievement, (4) originality and (5) expressiveness. The criteria are discussed individually and summarized in the music evaluation form (Figure 12-4).

Complexity and challenge. Good music, like a good friend, can be hard to get to know at first. Serious music is often quite complex, requiring intensive practice to bring it up to a reasonable performance level. Students cannot comprehend the work in the early rehearsals. They only learn to hate it. They must be cautioned to defer judgment until they actually hear the completed performance. However, there is an easier solution. After reading the composition through and rehearsing it for a reasonable length of time, play a good recording of it. The reaction is usually unbelievable—"So that's how it's supposed to sound." "Wow! That's really not such a bad number."

Complexity also means that a composition is musically and/or technically challenging. In its way it is hard to play. A Bach chorale presents a musical challenge. The Hindemith *Symphony* presents a musical and a technical challenge.

Lasting Interest and Value. Some students judge a composition by the question, "Is the composer dead?" If he is deceased, the music is not good. The fact that it has lasted for years, however, indicates that good music continues to carry a message—it is still relevant. People keep finding meaning in it over the years. An individual student can keep finding something more in a good composition each time it is replayed. It sustains interest by its complexity or subtlety. Students do not tire of it. This process can be likened to a series of car rides over the same route. The first time, the perceptive passenger gets a general impression of the landscape. If he pays attention each time the route is traversed, more things are noticed. He forms a clearer and more complete picture.

Most directors verify that students want to repeat the better music from year to year. Students quickly tire of the trite. Good music wears well. Commercial music of all types is written for mass consumption and entertainment. Since it emphasizes novelty and effect to "catch on," it may be extremely popular for a period of time, but, it eventually fades from the musical scene. It has no lasting value.

Technical Achievement. A good piece of music is well put together. It exhibits the knowledge and skill of a master composer. He knows how to handle the materials and elements of music. The form is an expressive integration and development of the elements.

Originality. The music is unique and imaginative. It is not obvious, cliché or trite. However, it is not just "novel." It seems right and necessary in the sense that it cannot be improved upon.

Expressiveness. The music presents patterns of intensity to release in tonal motion as described in Chapter 10.

Figure 12-4

STANDARDS FOR JUDGING MUSIC

Yes	No	
___	___	Complexity and/or challenge
___	___	Lasting interest and value
		Do not tire of it _____
		Find something new in it each time it is played _____
___	___	Technical Achievement
		Skill of composer with orchestration, elements and
		structure: _____
		Use of instruments _____
		Rhythm _____
		Melody _____
		Harmony _____
		Form _____
		elements integrated _____
		elements developed _____
___	___	Originality
___	___	Expressiveness

13

How to Evaluate
Musicianship

After a program of musicianship has been implemented, the curious and competent band director will want to know how well it is going. This can be done in an informal way. He can organize his curriculum, try it out, and simply "see how it works." How successful is it? Does the group respond favorably to it? Are they learning anything? Does the group perform better? Informal observation may not result in accurate assessment, although observation is one good method of evaluation.

Formal "testing" is another method of evaluation. Testing to determine student progress provides the director with an objective basis for grading bandsmen. The band program is often criticized for a certain subjectivity in this regard. However, formal testing tends to be limited to factual knowledge or performance skills. It is singularly incomplete since evaluation includes more than the terminal function of providing marks at the end of a semester.

Continuous and comprehensive evaluation has an important diagnostic role when the results of measurement are used for student guidance. The student is made aware of personal strengths and weaknesses, and is provided with a feedback of information necessary for self-improvement. For the director, the most important use of evaluation is to ascertain the extent of student learning and to determine the effectiveness of his teaching.

In this chapter, tests are developed to evaluate the musicianship curriculum that has been outlined in Chapters 2 through 11. The approach is illustrative rather than comprehensive. It is intended to provide guidelines which can be adapted to the director's individual situation. Tests appropriate for evaluating musicianship include (1) information examinations, (2) listening examinations, (3) performance scales, (4) out-of-class tests and reports, and (5) individual performance tests.

INFORMATION EXAMINATIONS

The easiest type of test to give is a paper and pencil test of musical knowledge. This is hardly appropriate to a course in musicianship. "Musicianship" refers to the comprehensive understanding and application of musical concepts and skills in performance. However, the first step in concept formation is to label the concept to be learned, and define it to the best of one's ability in order to be able to use it. The concept of *staccato* is a good illustration. Most students are familiar enough with the term to define it as "short." Now they are able to use it. They demonstrate a "clipped," "chopped," percussive articulation. Yet, *staccato* means much more than this initial, faulty conception. Experience with different types and styles of music will bring about further discrimination. Correct interpretation of *staccato* depends upon such variables as tempo, dynamic level, historical style, instruments used, size of group and even the acoustics of the hall.

Only significant information should be tested. Separate necessary knowledge from "retrieval data." For example, most of the Italian markings can be "looked up" rather than memorized. The following listings illustrate the types of questions appropriate for assessing musicianship.

Styles

1. Define *marcato, staccato, legato* and *tenuto.*
2. Match style periods with the following statements by writing the correct letter in the space provided. (answers: B—Baroque, C—Classical, R—Romantic, M—Modern)
   a. The "symphonic poem" is a form of the <u>R</u> era.
   b. The *"concerto grosso"* is a form of the <u>B</u> era.
   c. Symmetrical formal organization is typical of the <u>C</u> period.
   d. The idea that a single composition or movement should embody only a single mood (or "affection" as it was called) was prevalent in the <u>B</u> era.
   e. Theme transformation was used as an important unifying device in the <u>R</u> era.
   f. Jazz has influenced serious music of the <u>M</u> era.
   g. Program music is typical of the <u>R</u> era.
   h. The <u>C</u> era has a light, delicate, refined style.
   i. Emotionalism, sentiment and subjectivity are characteristic of the <u>R</u> period.
   j. The fugue developed in the <u>B</u> period.
   k. The "sonata-allegro" form developed in the <u>C</u> era.
   l. Long, florid, sequential melodic lines are typical of the <u>B</u> period.
   m. The minuet is a characteristic form of the <u>C</u> era.
   n. "Figured bass *(basso continuo)* is found in the <u>B</u> era.
3. Outline the characteristics of the major historical styles: Baroque, Classical, Romantic, Contemporary. Include dates of each style.
4. Compare the Baroque with the Classical style.
5. Compare the Classical with the Romantic style.
6. Compare the Romantic with the Contemporary style.

Form

1. Outline the standard binary forms (design and tonal structure).
2. Outline the standard ternary form.
3. Outline rondo forms.
4. Outline the sonata-allegro form.
5. The basic, symmetrical formal design is A B A. <u>True</u> False
6. Repetition by imitation is the organizing principle of the <u>d</u> (a) sonata, (b) symphonic poem, (c) minuet, (d) fugue, (e) none of these.

7. The sonata-allegro form has three main sections: the exposition, the development and the c. (a) trio, (b) coda, (c) recapitulation, (d) repetition, (e) introduction.

8. In the sonata-allegro form the first theme group usually contrasts with the second theme group. True False

9. An extension which is added to the end of a musical composition to enhance the feeling of resolution and finality is called a d. (a) *da capo,* (b) trio, (c) recapitulation, (d) coda, (e) none of these.

10. Theme transformation refers to the musical technique of changing the expression or mood of a theme while retaining its musical shape. True False

11. List the five organizing principles of music.

12. The first movement of a symphony is usually in d form. (a) binary (b) ternary (c) rondo (d) sonata-allegro (e) none of these.

13. Repetition of formal sections must be exact to achieve formal coherence. True False

14. In an extended composition, comprehension and understanding depend upon remembering and recognizing the d. (a) program, (b) rhythms, (c) harmony, (d) themes (e) texture.

Fundamentals and elements of music

1. Write and/or identify all major and minor key signatures.
2. Identify meter signatures of examples provided.
3. Identify note names of treble, bass, tenor and alto clefs.
4. Give note values of examples provided.
5. Give rest values of examples provided.
6. Write out all major scales.
7. Write out all minor scales in natural, harmonic and melodic forms.
8. Build major triads from given roots.
9. Build minor triads from given roots.
10. Identify and/or write cadences.
11. Mark phrases by identifying cadences.
12. A cadence is a point of musical repose. True False
13. The texture of a single, unaccompanied melody is called c. (a) rough, (b) thin, (c) monophonic, (d) polyphonic, (e) homophonic.

14. To "modulate" means to move from one key or tonality to another. <u>True</u> False
15. A fugue is a good example of <u>c</u> texture. (a) monophonic (b) homophonic, (c) polyphonic.

Timbre and instrumentation

1. How do you get a good sound on your instrument? (Include breath support, embouchure, mouthpiece, and condition and quality of the instrument in your answer.)
2. Transpose the written parts to concert pitch in the given examples.
3. Transpose the concert pitch to written parts in the given examples.

Performance

1. Define the following elements of performance: intonation, balance, blend, technique.
2. What is meant by articulation? Give examples.
3. Why are dynamics important?

Expressive elements

1. How is music expressive?
2. What is meant by "line"?
3. What are the expressive elements?
4. The climax of a melody or composition is the point of highest intensity or tension. <u>True</u> False
5. Dissonance to consonance is harmonic tension to resolution. <u>True</u> False

LISTENING EXAMINATIONS

The listening examination is one of the most effective methods for teaching and evaluating discrimination in music. It helps develop musicianship and evaluate musicianship better than the information examination. Band music can be presented initially this way. Listening can be directed to the elements and form before it is played by the band. An opposite approach can be taken also. The band can listen to recordings of music it is rehearsing. Then the director can ask questions about it. The questions can be quite informal and unstructured initially—what do you hear? Sequences? Repetitions? Variations? Instruments? The questions can be directed next to elements and form.

1. What is the meter?
2. Describe the rhythm. (syncopated? cross rhythms?)
3. Describe the melody. (diatonic? chromatic? disjunct?)
4. What is the theme (or themes)?
5. Describe the harmony. (dissonant? diatonic? chromatic?)
6. Is it tonal or atonal music?
7. Do you hear modulations?
8. What is the predominant texture?
9. What is the form?
10. What is the historical style?
11. If two compositions are compared, which is better? Why?
12. Which performance is better? Why?

For formal testing, use an examination form as Figure 13-1.

PERFORMANCE SCALES

The rating scales in Chapter 10 can be used to determine the ability of students to discriminate musical performance, performance of styles and the worth of music. Reference has been made earlier to the use of rating scales by students at competition festivals. This puts students to work. It gets them out of the halls and into the performances. Evaluation is complete when you check their ratings against yours and, if possible, the actual adjudicators ratings.

The scales can be used in another way. Invite a colleague to evaluate your group in rehearsal and/or performance to determine how well your group is progressing in musicianship prior to festival.

OUT-OF-CLASS TESTS AND REPORTS

Many student study sheets and analyses have been developed in the proposed curriculum. These can form the basis of initial out-of-class assignments. Additional research can be assigned as the musicianship program is expanded. Both written reports and oral reports of this research are appropriate. A good stock of reference books is necessary. The following outline illustrates assignments for developing and evaluating musicianship.

Figure 13-1

LISTENING QUIZ FOR BAND

Group	Tonality	Basic Meter	Texture	Historical Style
Band	Major	In one	Monophonic	Baroque
Orchestra	Minor	In two	Homophonic	Classical
Brass Choir	Modal	In three	Polyphonic	Romantic
Woodwind Quintet	Atonal or 12 tone	In four		Contemporary
1	1	1	1	1
2	2	2	2	2
3	3	3	3	3
4	4	4	4	4
5	5	5	5	5
etc.				

1. Research and written reports on research.
   a. History of the student's instrument.
   b. Biography of a composer.
   c. Report of a historical style period.
   d. Report on a formal type.

    e. Report on a musical element.

    f. Analysis of a composition (elements and form).

2. Written program notes for a concert.
3. Book reports on relevant books about music history, form, theory and/or expression.
4. Record listening and listening reports.
   a. Music being performed (as the original orchestral version of a transcription).
   b. A specific musical style.
   c. A comparison of musical styles.
   d. A specific form.
   e. An instrument.
5. Theory
   a. Harmony assignments of all types.
   b. Analysis of cadences.
   c. Composition.
6. Arranging
   a. Develop a chart of transpositions and ranges of the standard band instruments.
   b. Arrange a work for band or for an ensemble.

INDIVIDUAL PERFORMANCE TESTS

The applied examination is the "true" test of musicianship. Here the bandsman demonstrates his musicianship on his performing medium. The applied exam can be a natural part of the tryout, sectional rehearsal, or preparation of solo and ensemble for festival. Students can do much of the preparation individually by using the check lists and study sheets developed with the musicianship curriculum. The applied examination can include any or all of the following items that are demonstrated in performance:

1. Tone
2. General styles
3. Historical styles
4. Expression (phrasing)
5. Technique
   a. Scales (keys, tonality)
   b. Chords (arpeggios)
   c. Rhythm patterns

   d. Note and rest values (sight reading ability can be assessed
      with the Watkins-Farnum Performance Scales, pub. Hal
      Leonard)

14

How to Sell a Musicianship
Program to the
Administration and Students

Space-age priorities, changing values, curriculum reform and crises in educational financing have drastically altered the traditional place of the band in the high school. Band programs are fighting for their very existance in some school systems. Schools are dropping complete music programs because of financial difficulties and current educational priorities. How can the band program be saved? The musicianship curriculum as outlined in this book can be a step toward the solution. It provides a solid justification for band in the curriculum. To this end, the final chapter is devoted to selling the idea of a musicianship program to administration and students.

SELLING THE PROGRAM TO THE ADMINISTRATION

Administrators can be assured that none of the traditional values of the band will be lost. The band will function as usual and keep all reasonable commitments. The band can entertain at football games, march in parades, and continue to work as the public relations arm of the front office. The band will still promote citizenship, health, social adjustment, worthy use of leisure time, *ad infinitum*. The important point is that the band will move beyond these often superficial, noneducational and certainly nonmusical goals.

The proposed curriculum emphasizes music as a fine art or cultural, aesthetic study. The importance of aesthetic education as one facet of the development of the total person has been well stated by administrators themselves. According to a published document underwritten by the American Association of School Administrators, the central purpose of American education is to develop the ability to think.[1] Thinking includes rational, abstract and creative dimensions.

> . . . the abilities involved in perceiving and recognizing patterns in a mass of abstract data are of considerable importance in learning to analyze, deduce and infer. These abilities may be developed in the course of mathematical study; but this may be done as well through experiences in aesthetic, humanistic, and practical fields which also involve perception of formal design. Music, for example, challenges the listener to perceive elements of form within the abstract. . . .[2]

A viable curriculum has been developed. It consistently emphasizes the teaching of music and musicianship as the primary goal of the band program. It has content, continuity and evaluation. This answers the criticism of many administrators who argue that the band program really has no content since a student does essentially the same thing from one year to the next. In the musicianship curriculum, the individual student interacts with *music* which is an indispensable part of education.[3]

---

[1] *The Central Purposes of American Education.* (Washington, D.C.: Educational Policies Commision of NEA and American Association of School Administrators, 1961) p. 12.

[2] *Ibid,* pp. 17-18. Read the entire report for ammunition.

[3] *Music in the Senior High School.* (Washington, D.C.: Music Educators National Conference, 1959) p. 47.

A school band program which seeks to give the individual something of intrinsic worth through contact with an extensive repetoire, representing the best of the world's music, balanced by attention to theory, skill development and listening, can foster the kind of music appreciation and understanding that will be effective in the life of the individual in the school and in the community. Quality rather than quantity must receive the emphasis. The music experienced through the band must be of such a standard that it imparts lasting values. Music is then given an opportunity to play a major role all through life. The individual will be less likely to drop his instrument upon completion of his high school career, and even if he does not continue his own playing, his attitude toward music and culture generally will be sympathetic.[4]

The proposed curriculum can elevate band to the position of an academic subject. As a "solid" subject, additional credit and prestige would be warranted. Instead of administrators easing band out of the school curriculum, band should regain or retain its position as part of the regular school day. I have also experienced a positive change in the attitude of classroom teachers toward the band when they became aware that students were learning significant content of cultural value. The band gained respect as a member of the academic community.

The music appreciation assembly

The content of the entire book points toward the "Music Appreciation Assembly." The materials, forms and styles of music studied in rehearsal can be presented in an interesting way to the school, extending the influence of the band curriculum to the total student body. One good educational rule states that all performances should be an outgrowth of classroom learning activities. Our end product can be well displayed at assemblies that teach the general student about music. This reaches the "other 80%"—those students who do not take music in any form in the high school. Administrators will "appreciate" also. They appreciate the numbers of students that can be involved with the

---

[4] *Ibid.* Note also the "Four-Year Planned Band Program" of "Skill Development" appended to the book.

music program and the role the band can play in this total involvement.

The "Bernstein approach" is effective. The director discusses and analyzes music for form and style. (A narrator can be used if desired.) Finally, the complete composition is performed. Audio-visual aids can be used to great advantage—diagrams of forms, indications of theme entrances or important instruments, etc. Here are some possible examples.

1. Play the main themes from a composition and show how they are put together to create "form." The sonata-allegro design works well. The principal theme, subordinate theme and perhaps the closing theme are played and contrasted. Their use in the development can also be explained and demonstrated. The first movement of the Haydn *London Symphony* and the Beethoven *Egmont Overture* are good examples to use.
2. Contrast two historical styles, explaining the characteristics of each. Compare elements and forms. The band can play a melody from one and then from the other.
3. Concentrate upon the timbre of the band and its component instruments. Emphasize sounds and colors, singly and in combination.
4. Concentrate upon one or more of the musical elements. An assembly featuring "rhythms" can be exciting.

A series of assemblies can be lined up and promoted to parallel the study of the band curriculum. Clear assembly dates early.

The music appreciation concert

The community can benefit from this "extended" band curriculum in a similar way. I have found that the "history of musical style" results in an interesting program with excellent audience response, especially when lighter contemporary works are included at the program's end. Figure 14-1 is a high school band concert presented in 1959. Appropriate program notes were included. (See Chapter 8 for additional concert ideas and appropriate literature.) Concerts can include themes such as "The March Through the Ages," and "The *Concerto Grosso,* Then and Now."

Figure 14-1

TWO AND ONE-HALF CENTURIES OF MUSIC

Prelude and Fugue in D Minor	Johann Sebastian Bach (1685-1750)
Military Symphonie in F	Francois Joseph Gossec (1734-1829)

    I. Allegro Maestoso
   II. Larghetto
  III. Allegro

Gaite Parisienne	Jaques Offenbach (1819-1880)
Trauersinfonie	Richard Wagner (1813-1883)
Comedians Gallop	Dmitri Kabalevsky (1904-)
English Folk Song Suite	Ralph Vaughan Williams (1872-1957)

    I. March "Seventeen Come Sunday"
   II. Intermezzo "My Bonnie Boy"
  III. March "Folk Songs form Somerset"

Beguine for Band	Glenn Osser
Selected Marches	

SELLING THE PROGRAM TO STUDENTS

Unfortunately, student response may not be encouraging at first. They are not used to this approach and may not know how to "take it." At first they may resent the additional work and the intellectual disequalibrium. Furthermore, they may not know what you are trying to accomplish because band was never like this before. Careful explanation is necessary, especially relating to your expectation of student behavior. Acceptance of the program by students largely depends upon the enthusiasm and commitment of the director. He must be excited about the curriculum and what it will accomplish. Certainly, most students will go along with a director if he is "in." Here are some suggestions.

1. Carefully outline your objectives so students know what the program is about and what they are expected to accomplish.
2. Don't try to do too much at once. Gradually work into the program and keep expanding it from one year to the next.
3. Involve the students in the program. Help them plan what to study and play. Have them write up program notes, and plan assembly programs.

The results of the curriculum can be electrifying to the director. I well remember my first year in one job and the senior football star who played third horn in the band. He never seemed to take his music too seriously and retained a bored, sullen expression through many rehearsals. I kept waiting for him to drop. He stayed and much to my surprise told me at the annual band banquet that he had learned more *about* music in that one year than he had in all the other seven years combined. That alone made it all worthwhile.

General Index

A

Adjudicators comment sheet, 201-202
Administration, selling program to, 220-224
Aleatoric, 159
Analysis of music, 112-113
Arch form, 100
Arrangers, student, 34-35
Arranging "data sheet," 34
Articulation and style, 115-117
Assignments, 21-22
Asymmetrical meter, 45
Audio-visual materials, 22

B

Band director as teacher, 24-25
Band literature, selection, 16
Barbarism, 157
Baroque style:
    articulation, 126, 136-137
    Baroque era, 135-142
    compared to Classical, 178-185
    compositions, 139
    dynamics, 127, 137
    form, 138-139
    general characteristics, 135
    harmony, 136
    important composers, 139
    instrumentation, 137-138
    interpretation, 205
    melody 127, 135
    orchestration, 128
    ornamentation, 138
    projects, 139-142
    rhythm, 127, 136-137
    tempo, 127
    texture, 137
    tone, 127
Beat, 43, 48-52
"Bernstein" approach, 23, 223
Binary forms, 91-95

C

Cadence, 74-76
Characteristics, stylistic:
    Baroque compared to Classical, 178-185
    Classical compared to Romantic. 165-178
    elements and forms, 163
Chord construction, 73-74
Chromatic melody, 69
Classical style:
    articulation, 128
    Classical era, 142-147
    compared to Baroque, 178-185
    compared to Romantic, 165-178
    compositions, 147
    dynamics, 128, 145
    form, 146-147
    general characteristics, 142
    harmony, 143-144
    important composers, 147
    instrumentation, 145-146
    interpretation, 205
    melody, 129, 142-143
    orchestration, 129
    ornamentation, 146
    rhythm, 129, 144-145
    tempo, 129
    texture, 145
    tone, 129
"Common-elements" approach, 26
Compound meter, 58
Concerto grosso, 111-112, 133
Concerts, 223-224
Conductor as teacher, 24-25
Consonance, 77
Contemporary Music Project outline, 26
Contemporary period:
    composers, trends, compositions. 156-159
    dynamics, 155

Contemporary period (*cont.*)
  form, 156
  general characteristics, 154-155
  harmony, 155
  instrumentation, 156
  melody, 155
  projects, 159-161
  rhythm, 155
  texture, 155
Contemporary style, 130-131, 206
"Content," 24-25
Continuity, 24
Contrast, 87
Count, 43
Courses, music electives, 23
Curriculum, 24
Cyclic approach, 24

D

"Data sheet," arranging, 34
Demonstration, 22-23, 57-59
Diatonic melody, 67-69
Director as teacher, 24-25
Discrimination, musical, 200-210
Discussion, 22-23
Dissonance, 77
Dot, 58
Duration, 26

E

Electives, music subject, 23
Elements, musical
  (*see* Musical elements)
Ensemble drill, 18-19
Ensemble program and tone, 33-34
Evaluation:
  individual performance tests, 218-219
  information examinations, 212-215
  listening examinations, 215-216
  out-of-class tests and reports, 216-218
  performance scales, 216
Experimentalism, 159
Expression marks, 186-190
Expressionism, 157-158

F

Form:
  components and principles, 86-91
  contrast, 87
  definition, 86
  design, 87

repetition, 87
symmetry, 87
tonal structure, 88-91
types, 91-112
  arch, 100
  binary, 91-95
  concerto grosso, 111-112
  free, 112
  fugue, 108-111
  multiple, 112
  ostinato, 105-108
  rhondo, 96-100
  sonata-allegro, 102-105
  ternary, 96
  theme and variations, 100-102
Fugue, 108-111, 133

H

Harmony and texture:
  cadence, 74-76
  contemporary harmonic techniques, 79-80
    other harmonic devices, 80
    polytonality, 79
    serial harmony, 79-80
  dissonance and consonance, 77
  progression, 77-79
  texture, 80-85
    (*see also* Texture)
  tonality and chord construction, 73-74
Historical styles (*see also* under specific items):
  comparing musical characteristics, 162-185
  judging interpretation, 205-206
  musical characteristics, 134-161
  performance practice, 124-133
Homophonic Texture, 81-82

I

Impressionism, 157
Information, incidental, 19-20

J

Jazz, 158

L

Lecture, 22-23
Legato, 115, 117, 118, 119, 121, 188
Leggiero, 117

M

Marcato, 115, 117, 118, 119, 188
March, 122, 132
Melodic design, 67-69
Melody and theme:
  chromatic melody, 69
  diatonic structure and melodic design, 67-69
  motive, 66
  phrase, 66-67
  scales, 62-65
    rehearsal procedures, 63-65
    student projects, 63
    term, 62
  sequence, 66
  serial melody, 69-70
  theme, 70-71
  tonality, 61-62
MENC, 26
"Menu principle," 16
Meter, 43-44, 45-48
Mimeographed materials, 22
Mitropolis, Dimitri, 25
Monophonic Texture, 81
Motive, 66
Music:
  analysis, 112-113
  characteristics, stylistic, 162-185
    (*see also* Characteristics, stylistic)
  discrimination, 200-210
  "nonmetric" or "unmetric," 48
  presentation, 19-23
    (*see also* Presentation of music)
  selection, 16
  styles, 114-123
    (*see also* Styles)
  value judgments, 206-210
"Music Appreciation Assembly," 222-223
Musical characteristics (*see also* specific heading):
  Baroque period, 135-142
  Classical period, 142-147
  Contemporary period, 154-161
  Romantic period, 148-154
Musical elements (*see* under specific items):
  harmony and texture, 72-85
  melody and theme, 60-71
  rhythm, 42-59
Musicianship:
  evaluation, 211-219 (*see also* Evaluation)
  selling program, 220-225

N

Nationalism, 156-157
Neoclassicism, 158
Neoromanticism, 156
Nonmetric music, 48

O

Ostinato forms, 105-108
Outlines, 20
Overtures, dramatic, 131-132

P

Performance, judging, 201-204
Performance practice:
  Baroque style, 126-128
  Classical style, 128-129
  Contemporary style, 130-131
  defining and explaining, 124-131
  projects comparing, 131-133
    concerto grosso, 132
    dramatic overture, 131-132
    march, 132
    prelude and fugue, 133
  Romantic style, 129-130
Phrase, 66-67
Pianissimo, 117, 187
Pitch, 26
Polymeter, 44-45
Polyphonic Texture, 82-83
Polytonality, 79
Prelude, 133
Presentation of music:
  assign out-of-class study, 21-22
  distribute printed material, 20-21
  prepare program notes, 21
  provide incidental information, 19-20
  provide music subject electives, 23
  utilize class discussion, 22-23
Primitivism, 157
Printed material, 20-21
Program:
  notes, 21
  selling, 220-225
Progression, 77-79

Q

Quality, 26

R

Rehearsals, 17-19
  (*see also* Time and scheduling)
Repetition, 87

Rhythm:
  beat, 43
  changing meter, 45-48
  count, 43
  four basic concepts, 57
  meter, 43-44
  nonmetric music, 48
  polymeter, 44-45
  reading and interpreting, 48-54
    achieving evenness of runs, 53-54
    achieving rhythmic flow, 52-54
    counting divisions and subdivisions
      of beat, 49-52
    feeling beat units, 48-49
  student study sheet, 50, 51
  teaching in rehearsal, 56-59
    demonstration, analysis and drill
      experience, 57-59
    sight reading experience, 56
  uneven meter, 45
Romantic style:
  articulation, 129, 149
  compared to Classical, 165-178
  compositions, 151
  dynamics, 130, 149
  form, 150
  general characteristics, 148
  harmony, 148-149
  important composers, 150
  instrumentation, 149-150
  interpretation, 206
  melody, 130, 148
  orchestration, 130
  projects, 151-154
  rhythm, 130
  Romantic period, 148-154
  tempo, 130
  texture, 149
  tone, 130
Rondo, 96-100
Rubato, 122-123

S

Scales, 62-65
Scheduling, time and, 17-19
  (*see also* Time and scheduling)
Score:
  expression marks, 186-190
  musical structure and interpretation,
    190-199
  nature of musical expression, 190-
    191
  teaching phrase and line, 191-199

Selection of music, 16
Sequence, 66
Serial harmony, 79-80
Serial melody, 69-70
Serial music, 157-158
Shape, 26
Sight reading, 56
Simple meter, 58
Sonata, allegro, 102, 105
Sonority, 31-33
Sound, 26
Staccato, 115, 117, 118, 119, 121, 122,
  188
Students, selling program to, 224-225
Study guides, 20
Styles:
  articulation and style, 115-117
  basic, 117-120
  chart, 164
  historical, 124-185
    (*see also* Historical styles)
  legato, 115, 117, 118, 119, 120, 121,
    122
  leggiero, 117
  marcato, 115, 117, 118, 119, 121
  march, 122
  pianissimo, 117
  rubato, 122-123
  staccato, 115, 117, 118, 119, 120,
    121, 122
  symbols, 120-122
  Tenuto, 118, 121, 123
Symmetry, 87

T

Tenuto, 118, 121, 123, 188
Ternary forms, 96
Tests (*see* Evaluation)
Texture:
  homophonic, 81-82
  monophonic, 81
  polyphonic, 82-83
  several in one composition, 83-85
  terms, 80-81
Theme, 70-71
Timbre, teaching, 35-41
  (*see also* Tone)
Time and scheduling:
  ensemble drill, 18-19
  rehearsal management, 19
  warm-up and tuning, 17-18
Tonal structure, 88-91
Tonality, 61-62

Tone:
  ensemble program, 33-34
  rehearsal, 28-30
  workshop, 30-31
Tuning, warm-up and, 17-18

U

Uneven meter, 45
Unit, 58
Unmetric music, 48

V

Value judgments, 206-210
Variation, 100-102

W

Warm-up and tuning, 17-18
Woodbury, Ward, 24
Worksheets, 20
Written materials, 20

Index of

Musical Examples

B

Binary form, 93

C

"Chaconne" from Holst's *First Suite in E Flat*, 106
Concerto Grosso, 139, 141

D

"Dialogue" from *Miniature Set for Band*, 79

E

Egmont Overture, 76
English Folk Song Suite, 117-118

F

"Fifth Movement" *Dodecaphonic Set*, 81
Fifth Symphony, 66
"Finale" from *Suite in F for Band*, 46
Folk Song Suite, 44

H

"Hallelujah Chorus" from the *Messiah*, 76, 84

I

If Thou Be Near, 85
"Intermezzo" from *English Folk Song Suite*, 67, 194

J

Jupiter Symphony, 143

L

"Largo" from *New World Symphony*, 52-53, 68, 82
Les Preludes, 153
Little Fugue in G Minor, 62, 74
Londonderry Air, 92
"Lord Melbourne" from *Lincolnshire Posey*, 46, 48

M

March for the Prince of Wales, 143
"March" from *Folk Song Suite*, 52
"Mars" from *The Planets*, 45, 69
"Menuetto" from *Toy Symphony*, 144
Messiah Overture, 137, 138
Military Symphony for Band, 138

N

National Anthem, 61, 73

O

"Ode to Joy" theme from *Ninth Symphony*, 88
Overture in C, 104

P

Prelude and Fugue in D Minor, 64-65, 71, 82
Psyche and Eros, 77

Q

Quarter-note drills, 118

R

Rienzi Overture, 69, 78, 81

S

Scale patterns, major and minor, 62-63
Scale Tones, 65
"*Second Movement*" from *Lincoln-shire Posey,* 196
"*Second Movement*" from *Three Miniatures for Band,* 78, 80
"*Second Movement*", *Military Symphony in F,* 75
Second Suite, 63, 115-116

Second Suite in F, 45
"*Song of the Blacksmith*" from *Second Suite,* 56
"*Song Without Words*" from *Second Suite,* 53-54, 67, 192, 193, 197
St. Anthony Chorale, 66, 78
St. Anthony Divertimento, 143

T

Tapor No. 1 for Band, 83
Three Miniatures for Band, 70, 78, 80
"*Trio*" from *Stars and Stripes Forever,* 83

Y

Ye Banks and Braes O'Bonnie Doon, 43, 62, 75, 194, 195, 196